About the Author

Yemi Lufadeju, also known as The Beloved Daughter, is passionate about discovering and revealing God's heart. She speaks and writes about the tensions and victories of life in God's family in the twenty-first century. She serves in her local church in London, England, and supports a network of Christian groups as a speaker and ministry coordinator.

To find out more, visit thebeloveddaughter.com.

Family, The Divine Enterprise
Empowered for a Takeover

Yemi Lufadeju

Family, The Divine Enterprise
Empowered for a Takeover

Olympia Publishers
London

www.olympiapublishers.com
OLYMPIA PAPERBACK EDITION

Copyright © Yemi Lufadeju 2024

The right of Yemi Lufadeju to be identified as author of
this work has been asserted in accordance with sections 77 and 78 of
the Copyright, Designs and Patents Act 1988.

All Rights Reserved

No reproduction, copy or transmission of this publication
may be made without written permission.
No paragraph of this publication may be reproduced,
copied or transmitted save with the written permission of the publisher,
or in accordance with the provisions
of the Copyright Act 1956 (as amended).

Any person who commits any unauthorised act in relation to
this publication may be liable to criminal
prosecution and civil claims for damage.

A CIP catalogue record for this title is
available from the British Library.

ISBN: 978-1-80074-927-6

The information of this document expresses my personal views and
opinions and does not necessarily represent the views of any
organisation.

First Published in 2024

Olympia Publishers
Tallis House
2 Tallis Street
London
EC4Y 0AB

Printed in Great Britain

Dedication

To Gbolafunmi, sister, friend, confidant, alive in my heart, forever in my thoughts.

Acknowledgements

John Lufadeju, I'm convinced you are God's choice for me; doing life with you is evidence of His love, grace and mercy towards me. Thank you for being an enabling, encouraging and supportive husband. As amazing as our life together is, the best is yet to come.

Gbolahan Folayan, my father, number one fan and cheerleader. Every word of encouragement and affirmation has been a seed sown on fertile ground. You keep speaking light, life and truth over me and you will definitely eat from its bountiful harvest. Thank you for never giving up, for always supporting and investing in who God says I am. You are a wonderful expression of what being a good father is; thank you for raising me as a beloved daughter, I love you.

Grace Folayan, mum, I've been watching you all my life and through you I see truly that grace is God's empowering presence. You truly are an overcomer and you've raised me as such. Your unrelenting prayers and counsel have come from a place of love and commitment to our family. I pray you receive to yourself a bountiful harvest for every sacrifice you've made for your children. I pray with this harvest comes the joy of God's redeeming and restorative love, grace and mercy.

Gbolabo Folayan, a family man like no other. Your heart for family is inspiring. You echo Father's heart for the unity, loyalty and purpose expected in each one of us. Being your sister is like winning the lottery every day, because you've always got my back.

Folashade and Gbolade my wonderful sisters. Our childhood was full of awe and wonder. You are both key characters in my faith story. Individually, you led me to Christ and showed me what being committed to God's love looks like. Through incredible hardship, I've seen you both cling to your faith, be it through valleys shadowed by death, or faced by mountainous problems, your resolve, resilience and perseverance is remarkable. I'm grateful to you.

Valerie Elyott, thank you for modelling so beautifully what it looks like to be loved by God, to abide and be in His presence. Your passion for intimacy with our Father is contagious. Thank you for sharing this with me; it has changed my life forever.

Dorothy Sadoh, you've made a brilliant impression on me. Thank you for your contributions to this work. Serving alongside you in the Elyott Generation has been a blessing.

Introduction
Why this Book is Relevant

Imagine for a moment that Family is a global enterprise and God is the founder who sits on the board with all control and power...

Let's call it the Divine Enterprise – a global self-sustaining entity that produces and supports a workforce of skilled and equipped experts with shared interests in expanding God's empire. Not just for His enrichment, but as their eternal inheritance.

Continue to stretch your imagination with the thought that God is very hands-on, so much so He appoints His Son, Jesus, as Chief Executive and puts His Spirit to work as the Chief Operating Officer. Together, they make the formidable force called The Trinity. They adopt each family, declaring them no-longer slaves but sons and daughters.

Together, the Trinity pour their heart into each family, investing unsparingly in training and developing this workforce that will one day be a powerful monopoly across the world.

A Means to an End
Can you imagine this? Does it sound familiar? Perhaps not, because many in this family are unaware of their identity, purpose, power and authority, and there's opposition to

make sure this ignorance continues unchallenged.

There are competing forces at work which seek to distort the true narrative of family. These forces try to confine the divine enterprise to the things of fairy tales and fiction defined by sorrow, grief and conflict such that the truth seems unrealistic and too good to be true.

The competing force – let's call it The Conglomerate – is determined to break families. This is because it's fully aware that the families' potential to succeed is rooted in their knowledge of their identity as beloved sons and daughters of God and in their oneness and unity with the Trinity – collectively and individually. To break families is to win the ultimate battle which is to deny God the fulfilment of His purpose of expanding and establishing His Kingdom with people.

Thankfully, nothing takes the Trinity by surprise.

Incredibly, the heart of the Father – God, is such that establishing His Kingdom is a means to an end. The real victory, God's true desire is for the people. Building an everlasting Kingdom is a shared purpose towards His everyday passion – relationship, intimacy with each son and daughter.

For every day He gets to have this, He has already won. He started victorious and will never be overcome, so The Conglomerate is fighting a non-battle, losing every day, too arrogant, diabolic and ignorant to ever comprehend this.

Relationship with the Trinity is the victory.

The Special Operatives
Aware of the opposition, but never deterred by it, the Trinity is unrelenting in their investment in each family. For each one, the first victory is the discovery of purpose and

identity, adoption in the Family, the Divine Enterprise.

Strategies are devised to recruit those that are still in the orphanages of life and help them feel at home in the Family. Nothing is hidden from the Father, every hurt, pain, deficiency of the heart, malady of the soul is seen and will be healed.

Everyone in the Divine Enterprise is destined to succeed. No investment is spared to strengthen them in their growth, development, maturity and prosperity. The resources, equipment, skills, gifts they need to thrive are readily available.

Each one has a clearly defined role as a special operative. Each one is appointed to function effectively and successfully within the family framework of dad, mum, grandparent, godparent, guardian, mentor, sibling, aunt, uncle, sons, daughters, nieces, nephews, godchildren, protégés and protégées.

Family, The Divine Enterprise – Adoption is equal to Identity

Here's the thing, for each operative to successfully function in their role, they must know God as Father, believe that Jesus is His Son and receive the Holy Spirit. This makes God's fatherhood real to them, affirms their identity and enables them to grow and mature as children of God.

For family to work, everyone must believe, agree with, and receive their adoption as God's children. The moment they sincerely do, the process of victorious living begins. There goes the tension, the pressure, fear and burden of being family. Here comes the joy, delight, favour and grace of being in God's Family – the Divine Enterprise.

Parented by God

As each special operative grows and matures as a child of God, parented by God, they start to fulfil their potential. As Jesus walks alongside each one, their excellence radiates God's goodness effortlessly, life has meaning, and vision articulates purpose. Through the Holy Spirit, each operative complements the other (when they yield and surrender to the process of being family) to shine in their uniqueness, inevitably glorifying God the Father.

When families submit to being parented by God, a beautiful cycle of life is established never to be broken when God's children are raising God's children.

Find Yourself Here

Regardless of your story, there's a place for you in this eternal enterprise called Family. Despite loss, abuse, disappointment, disgrace, abandonment, rejection or being disowned, God has made a place for you in His Family. He invites you to believe, agree with and receive His adoption of you as His child. He wants you to accept His love with no strings attached.

Can you see yourself as loved? Will you allow Him to parent you? Find yourself in Him, there's a seat for you at His table, draw near, come in.

God's word is one of the major resources we have for locating ourselves in The Divine Enterprise. It reveals our identity, and it introduces us to God; it helps build our faith and serves as guard rails of trust, discipline, growth and maturity, protecting us from the relentlessly diabolic strategies of The Conglomerate. In the Word of God, we find direction, guidance and insight that help us discover purpose and fulfil our potential. There's no substitute for it.

Prayer and declarations of God's word are key to living out our purpose as Special Operatives within the Divine Enterprise. In the following pages, we'll find references to scriptures that'll help us navigate some of those situations that come our way. They'll help us prepare for and overcome those tricks of The Conglomerate to sabotage our families and steal us away from the Divine Enterprise.

These prayers and declarations are like tools in our hands and will help keep us faithful, committed and focused on our purpose. They will keep our eyes on the main thing that defines our victory – relationship with God, fellowship with The Trinity and intimacy that grows stronger and remains unbroken.

The journey ahead may not be easy, but one spiritual fact we must hold on to is that ultimately, we start victorious and remain victorious when we remain in The Trinity.

Being Beloved
There is very little about love that is passive. We need to open ourselves up to be loved and open our minds and hearts to being loved; and it could take a while to accept this as a lived reality.

One major deception of The Conglomerate is the thought that love can be demanded and is passive, that it just happens. The concept of 'falling in love' or 'love at first sight' are all distortions of the real thing, distortions from the truth that love really is a person – Jesus, the Son of God.

Within the family structure, to love is a choice; to take on the personality and characteristics of Jesus. Love is not passive; it should be active, intentional and premeditated.

We choose to love and be loved, regardless of our difficulties, challenges, flaws and shortcomings – or that of others. To be loved is also to choose to be vulnerable and open to receive the love of others.

Many books have been written about love and relationships but of all these books, there is one book, The Bible, it exposes love from cover to cover. It will take a lifetime to fully comprehend its message, but it is perpetually enlightening and revealing of who true Love is. Distilling its message to a simple message really is to describe it as a love story. It speaks of the love of God for humanity and unpacks the heart-breaking trauma of separation from the object of His affection – man- unveiling His fiery passion and desire in a timeless pursuit for reconciliation and requited love from the very heart of the ones He created.

Right from day one, God's passion birthed humanity with the purpose of fellowship, community and family. That desire still burns for us. He has not given up, and for every person who draws breath, there's a call, an invitation to a deep and intimate relationship with the creator of the universe Himself.

I know for some, it may all sound far-fetched and difficult to comprehend, but our unbelief doesn't make it any less true. Personally, I , have struggled with the concept of love. It wouldn't be an exaggeration to say that it's taken divine intervention to open my mind, heart, and soul to the truth that Love is a person. This is the foundation, the bedrock of my faith – that God is love, Jesus is the personification of God's love, and I am the focus of His love. It's a mind-blowing thought and it gets me every time

I realise that this love of God is incredible, beyond description, inexplicable, unbreakable and undeniable. My eyes have been opened to catch a glimpse of how intense this love is. The moment I chose to believe it, I was tempted to accept this love and receive it in my heart and my entire life and world view changed.

To accept the love of God is to respond to the invitation to intimacy. For me, it was a leap of faith, like jumping into the abyss and hoping to be caught. Where I stood, all I could see was darkness, but what a glorious thing it was to be caught in the very instant I took a leap. There was no free-falling or fear or anxiety; never has trusting been so freeing, so reassuring, so affirming.

Jesus answered: *"Don't you know me, Philip, even after I have been among you such a long time? Anyone who has seen me has seen the Father. How can you say, 'Show us the Father'? Don't you believe that I am in the Father, and that the Father is in me?"*

"The words I say to you, I do not speak on my own authority. Rather, it is the Father, living in me, who is doing his work. Believe me when I say that I am in the Father and the Father is in me; or at least believe on the evidence of the works themselves." (John 14: 9-11 NIV)

Like Philip, some of us may have been hanging out with Jesus; perhaps we're familiar with Him, but haven't really gotten to connect with Him based on His true identity. It's likely there's still a hesitation to take that leap of faith; we're walking tentatively around Him, with Him but not fully given to Him. Let Love take you on a journey and win your heart. I encourage you to be open.

Choosing to believe, accept and receive God's love is

my daily response to Christ adopting me into the family of God. I was an orphan scrambling around in the big, dark ugly world and Jesus picked me up, cleaned me up and adopted me. With this adoption came identity. He gave me a name, purpose for being and a whole new life to live. The old me was dead and buried and this new creature was reborn and brought into the light of this glorious Kingdom.

As my eyes adjust to the brightness of His light, His Spirit reveals to me who I am. Every day brings new revelation of who this new creature is. Christ is introducing me to me, patiently working within the capacity of understanding I have while stretching me and growing me. It's a wonderful way to live; every day is exciting, making the choice to fit the uniquely perfect mould He's crafted with my name on it, is like nothing else.

Being loved is heaven on earth; it's literally living a life where God's Kingdom is made real. His reality is my reality.

It's tempting to want to interrupt this with a bubble-bursting statement of when things hit rock bottom and how there are sad and bad days when I don't necessarily feel God's love. But that would be disingenuous, misleading and a disservice to what His love is and what it means to be a beloved son or daughter of God.

"For this reason [grasping the greatness of this plan by which Jews and Gentiles are joined together in Christ], I bow my knees [in reverence] before the Father [of our Lord Jesus Christ], from whom every family in heaven and on earth derives its name [God—the first and ultimate Father]. May He grant you out of the riches of His glory, to be strengthened and spiritually energised with power through

His Spirit in your inner self, [indwelling your innermost being and personality], so that Christ may dwell in your hearts through your faith. And may you, having been [deeply] rooted and [securely] grounded in love, be fully capable of comprehending with all the saints (God's people) the width and length and height and depth of His love [fully experiencing that amazing, endless love]; and [that you may come] to know [practically, through personal experience] the love of Christ which far surpasses [mere] knowledge [without experience], that you may be filled up [throughout your being] to all the fullness of God [so that you may have the richest experience of God's presence in your lives, completely filled and flooded with God Himself]." (Ephesians 3:14-19 AMP)

Let's be clear – LOVE NEVER FAILS. Nothing on earth can ever take His love away, nothing can ever overcome God's love. It's the safety net of all safety nets and it's the assurance, comfort blanket for life. You need to receive this love to get the incredible difference it makes to life.

There will be turmoil and turbulence in life, whether you accept Love or not, it is a guaranteed fact of life. With Love in your life, that is Jesus, perspectives change, every pain and hurt and challenge is no longer yours but His to overcome. There's grace – God's empowering presence, which gives you the potential to go from a mere human to a supernatural being, doing the incredible.

No longer are we slaves to the destruction and devastation of being in this world. As beloved sons and daughters of God living life on His terms, seated in heavenly places with His Son, we get to look down on these challenges with the clarity that comes with the Wisdom released from the very throne of God.

Kingdom perspectives shed light on the darkness around us, our heart illuminated, and our words and actions manifest the life and truth they are designed to deliver. With this power and authority, we really have one thing to expect- victory.

It is true, the enemy will stop at nothing to prevent us from fully embracing God's love because he understands it's potential. Imagine again if one person in a family were to fully embrace God's love, it could totally transform generations to come. Think about what could happen when an entire family is fully immersed in the revealing, empowering, enlightening reality of God's love. Can you imagine? Communities, cities, nations would be transformed completely.

So, we must settle in our hearts that being loved by God is not a self-serving pursuit. God's love for us is not just about making us feel good, which it does, but it's about so much more. It's a living experience that has potential to give life and speak into generations to come. Being loved is not just an awareness, it's a state of being and a way of life that frames and determines mindsets, choices, character, values and principles.

Accepting God's Love, Jesus, determines whether we are just aware of God, or in a healthy and intimate relationship with Him, knowing Him through lived experiences. It is a choice between living the fullness of life in Christ, or as the living-dead in the world succumbing to sin's impact of guilt and condemnation. The choice is ours to make every day.

Scripture-Based Prayers and Declarations as Beloved Sons and Daughters of God

"Remember your word to your servant, for you have given me hope. My comfort in my suffering is this; Your promise preserves my life." (Psalm 119:49-50 NIV)

Being the beloved daughter or son of God is being firmly rooted in God's family, giving no room or opportunity to being displaced, uprooted or deceived about our identity, authority, purpose and inheritance.

Children of God have the privilege of direct access to the Father through prayer. Like the psalmist, we can find comfort in taking God's Word to Him from a place of relationship, intimacy, and trust. It's not because God has forgotten His word, but more-so for our benefit because doing this affirms our faith and is a source of comfort to us in both good and challenging times, serving as assurance of His promises.

Declarations and scripture-based prayers align us with the Holy Spirit who fills us with the confidence we need to stand firm and rooted in God's presence and love.

"...the Advocate, the Holy Spirit, whom the Father will send in my name, will teach you all things and will remind you of everything I have said to you. Peace I leave with you; my peace I give you. I do not give to you as the world gives. Do not let your hearts be troubled and do not be afraid." (John 14:25 NIV)

I invite you to read these scripture-based prayers and declarations. They have seen many through life's ups and downs, anchoring them in a place of faith. Note though, that they are not prescriptive. Consider them a guide for your prayers and your intimate conversations with God, see them as inspiration to thumb through the scriptures and read through the chapters and verses yourself, and attentively listen as the Holy Spirit informs your prayers.

We can trust the Holy Spirit as we do this because, *"the Spirit helps us in our weakness. We do not know what we ought to pray for, but the Spirit himself intercedes for us through wordless groans. And he who searches our hearts knows the mind of the Spirit, because the Spirit intercedes for God's people in accordance with the will of God."* (Romans 8:26 NIV)

This is a resource to equip us in prayer – which is essentially communication with God the Father, The Son and the Holy Spirit. Use it as a resource to ground you in position of strength and confidence in your identity as adopted and beloved, and to boldly approach your Father and speak in agreement with His heart for you.

Each section references Bible verses to inform prayers, stir faith and most importantly, encourage us to keep our focus on God. The purpose of this resource is to nurture our relationship with God, to equip us to keep on exploring God's Word and listen to the Holy Spirit as He reveals God's truth.

The Holy Spirit has been instructed to guide us in all truth; He has been authorised to help us develop our own prayer strategies to ensure we pray God's will. This resource helps us yield to that work of God in our lives, to lead us on to spiritual maturity and to fulfil God's purpose for our lives, as individuals and collectively as family.

As you read and pray through, may your heart be rekindled with a fresh desire for the Lord as you are reminded of His goodness, faithfulness, and love.
In Jesus name.
Amen.

Contents

Section 1: Grace, Forgiveness and Repentance

Section 2: The Family
- Prayers for the Whole Family
- Prayers and Declarations for Men: Grace, Wisdom and Power
- Prayers and Declarations for Mothers: Identity, Grace and Love
- Prayers and Declarations for Children: Destiny, Character, Purpose, and God's will

Section 3: Healing
- Prayers and Declarations on Healing and Deliverance: Faith, Forgiveness, and Life

Section 4: Business, Education, Finances
- Prayers over Finances: Faith, Humility, and Trust
- Prayers over Businesses/ Careers
- Prayers over Education

Section 5: Declarations for Sound Mental Health
- Declarations of Identity
- Declarations of Purpose
- Declarations of Authority and Power

Section 6: Aligning with God's Agenda
- Prayers for the Church: Unity, Love, and the Father's Heart…
- Prayers for Spiritual Leaders: Protection, Wisdom, Grace

Section 7: Praise, Worship, Thanksgiving

Section 1
Grace, Forgiveness and Repentance

God's love for humanity is expressed in many ways. From the moment He spoke the earth into being, formed man and set His redemption plan in motion, God's love continues to echo through the ages calling us into relationship with Him.

Jesus amplifies this message. His life on earth was the embodiment of this invitation – God's Kingdom is here, enter in. Through His sacrifice, He presented a new covenant between man and God, one where those who believe in Him would be adopted as sons and daughters of the Most High God, no longer destined for the penalty of sin – death. Through Jesus, we become partakers in the heritage of the righteous, with access to all God's Kingdom has to offer.

"My prayer is not that you take them out of the world but that you protect them from the evil one. They are not of the world, even as I am not of it. Sanctify them by the truth; your word is truth. As you sent me into the world, I have sent them into the world. For them I sanctify myself, that they too may be truly sanctified." (John 17:16-18 NIV).

So as God's children we are sanctified and sent to the world as ambassadors of Christ (2 Corinthians 5:16-21). He has given us a purpose and equipped us with everything we need to live a life of holiness and godliness to represent our heavenly Father and brother. But we're cautioned, it will not be without challenges and opposition.

"Be sober, be vigilant; because your adversary the devil walks about like a roaring lion, seeking whom he may devour. Resist him, steadfast in the faith, knowing that the same sufferings are experienced by your brotherhood in the world. But may the God of all grace, who called us to His eternal glory by Christ Jesus, after you have suffered a while, perfect, establish, strengthen, and settle you. To Him be the glory and the dominion forever and ever. Amen." (1 Peter 5:8-11 NKJV).

So, as we live driven by an eternity with God, our hearts must be focused on the desires and purpose of God's Kingdom. This is made known to us through the Spirit of God deposited in us.

Receiving God's salvation means embracing His grace and forgiveness for a life at odds with Him. We know we can boldly approach the throne of grace and make our confessions to a loving King who we get to call father. We take responsibility for our shortcomings and repent of them by being intentional and premeditated about never returning to those sins by His grace.

May your heart be full of God's love as you declare and affirm a relationship with Him.. As you pray these scriptures , I pray your heart is enlightened and your spirit aligned even stronger with the Holy Spirit as He strengthens and empowers you from the place of grace, mercy and love. In Jesus name.

"Therefore, with minds that are alert and fully sober, set your hope on the grace to be brought to you when Jesus Christ is revealed at his coming. As obedient children do not conform to the evil desires you had when you lived in

ignorance. But just as he who called you is holy, so be holy in all you do; for it is written: "Be holy, because I am holy." (1 Peter 1:13-16 NIV).

Prayers

- I don't want to be spiritually numb and ignorant, Holy Spirit, help me to be alert, fully sober, sharp and discerning.
- Help me live in the full awareness of who I am – a child of God and an ambassador of His Kingdom operating fully in my purpose, calling and the power and authority I have in Christ Jesus.
- I declare that I am an obedient child of God; I will not conform to worldly desires. I am dead to sin, a new creation in Christ Jesus. I have the Spirit of Christ in me and share the mind of Christ – sin has no hold on me. (Romans 8:3-4 KJV, 1 Corinthians 2:16 NKJV, 2 Corinthians 5:17 NIV)
- Lord, I choose to obey you and reject every evil desire that conflicts with your presence and lordship of my life.
- Holy Spirit, fix my heart on the hope of God's Grace through Jesus.
- Lord, I receive the grace to live in holiness and righteousness.
- Holy Spirit, enlighten my heart to make godly choices.

"For the grace of God has appeared that offers salvation to all people. It teaches us to say 'No' to ungodliness and worldly passions, and to live self-controlled, upright and godly lives in this present age,

while we wait for the blessed hope—the appearing of the glory of our great God and Saviour, Jesus Christ, who gave himself for us to redeem us from all wickedness and to purify for himself a people that are his very own, eager to do what is good." (Titus 2:11-14 NIV).

- Thank You, Lord, for your grace, which empowers me over sin and saves me from death.
- I receive Your grace to live in holiness and righteousness.
- I receive the wisdom, knowledge and understanding that comes with God's grace on my life to overcome temptation and sin.
- I confess that my life is godly, I am self-controlled, disciplined and upright by God's grace.

- I say, "No", to ungodliness now by the grace of God! When tempted, no one should say, *"God is tempting me." "For God cannot be tempted by evil, nor does he tempt anyone; but each person is tempted when they are dragged away by their own evil desire and enticed. Then, after desire has conceived, it gives birth to sin; and sin, when it is full-grown, gives birth to death. Don't be deceived, my dear brothers and sisters. Every good and perfect gift is from above, coming down from the Father of the heavenly lights, who does not change like shifting shadows. He chose to give us birth through the word of truth, that we might be a kind of first fruits of all he created."* (James 1:13-18 NIV).

- I renounce every evil desire that could drag me away from God. Holy Spirit, purge me of every conflicting desire that may entice my heart from the Lord.

- Lord, abort those evil desires in me that have grown into sin. Today I choose You and I reject those desires.
- Holy Spirit, I receive every good gift from God; sow seeds of the fruits of the Spirit in me; let them yield a bountiful harvest and leave no room for evil desires.
- Thank You, Lord, for every good gift you have sown in me.
- I declare that I am birthed of the Lord through the word of truth, and I will multiply and yield a bountiful harvest for God's kingdom.

"The end of all things is near. Therefore, be alert and of sober mind so that you may pray. Above all, love each other deeply, because love covers over a multitude of sins." (1 Peter 4:7-8 NIV).

- Help me, Holy Spirit, to live a life driven by an eternity with Christ.
- Bring my heart and mind back to focus on truth, to meditate on God's word and to hold on to it.
- I need the grace and stamina to pray heartfelt and fervent prayers; Thank You for Your love which redeems me from sin.
- Help me to love others in a redemptive and restorative way.

"Therefore, confess your sins to one another [your false steps, your offenses], and pray for one another, that you may be healed and restored. The heartfelt and persistent prayer of a righteous man (believer) is able to accomplish much [when put into action and made effective by God—it is dynamic and can have tremendous power]." (James 5:16 AMP).

- Lord, I admit my shortcomings and wrongdoing (be

specific); I'm sorry Lord, I choose to turn away from those actions and I declare that I want to live in right standing with You.
- I receive the healing and restoration that comes with confession and repentance.

"If we say that we have no sin, we deceive ourselves, and the truth is not in us. If we confess our sins, He is faithful and just to forgive us our sins and to cleanse us from all unrighteousness." (1 John 1:8-9 NKJV).

- Thank You, Father, because You love me, and You forgive my sin.
- Holy Spirit, help me make acceptable confessions.
- I receive the grace to offer persistent and heartfelt prayer; Lord, help me believe every confession, promise and declaration and live by Your Word.
- Thank You, Lord, because by Your grace I will accomplish much; You make me effective.
- Lord, help me pray dynamic and effective prayers that are backed by Your tremendous power. In Jesus name. Amen.

Section 2
The Family

No matter where you are in the world, you're likely to be familiar with news headlines of rising numbers of violent deaths of children and young people. You would have heard of abuses against children, of rising suicide rates, worries of their mental health and the many dangers they are susceptible to online.

No doubt you'll also be familiar with figures about divorce rates, and gender confusion. You may have seen multiple iterations of apps and online groups and communities marketed to solve the relationship problem and bring people together, be it for long-lasting connections, or fleeting sexual encounters.

Let it come as no surprise to you – there is an attack on families. The devil has been rolling out the same old strategy and it is simple and effective. Deception and manipulation have always been his tactics to make sure that society is fragmented and weak by corrupting and infiltrating families – the environment created as that initial introduction and access to our Heavenly Father. The enemy attacks the family to distort the reality and truth of love, identity, purpose, and authority. This tactic has been in his playbook since the dawn of time.

"But for Adam no suitable helper was found. So the Lord God caused the man to fall into a deep sleep; and

while he was sleeping, he took one of the man's ribs and then closed up the place with flesh. Then the Lord God made a woman from the rib he had taken out of the man, and he brought her to the man. The man said, *"This is now bone of my bones and flesh of my flesh; she shall be called 'woman,' for she was taken out of man." That is why a man leaves his father and mother and is united to his wife, and they become one flesh. Adam and his wife were both naked, and they felt no shame."* (Genesis 2:20-25 NIV).

Unity, oneness, trust, faith, hope and comfort were woven into marriage right from the start. This truth should be discovered and fully established in the family unit. But when brokenness sets in, the home is no longer that safe space to deliver the spiritual training, engagement, power, and authority that comes with the identity needed to live a life that pleases God. It is a clever plot, but our God is mighty and sovereign, and thankfully and mercifully, works things out for the good of those who love Him and are called according to His purpose (Romans 8:28 KJV).

In His wonderous way, He saves us despite the environment we are born into – no matter how damaging and imperfect. We can be confident of this, surely the enemy and his minions will gather and rally against families, but not by God, and He promises that they shall fall! (Isaiah 54:15-17 KJV). That is good news! God has provided a solution, Kingdom strategies to protect households from this corruption and degradation. As children of God, we have a duty to partner with Him as He continues to deliver His strategy for the restoration of families to His original design.

"What, then, shall we say in response to these things?

If God is for us, who can be against us? He who did not spare his own Son, but gave him up for us all—how will he not also, along with him, graciously give us all things? Who will bring any charge against those whom God has chosen? It is God who justifies. Who then is the one who condemns? No one. Christ Jesus who died—more than that, who was raised to life—is at the right hand of God and is also interceding for us. Who shall separate us from the love of Christ? Shall trouble or hardship or persecution or famine or nakedness or danger or sword?" (Romans 8:31-34 NIV).

Be determined that your household is a living response to that question, to say 'NO!', nothing shall separate us from the love of Christ. No matter what your family is like now, God affirms us with the truth that, therefore, there is now no condemnation for those who are in Christ Jesus... (Romans 8:1 NIV).

So, let us throw off everything that hinders and the sin that so easily entangles. And let us run with perseverance the race marked out for us, fixing our eyes on Jesus, the pioneer and perfecter of faith. (Hebrews 2:1-2 NIV)

It is important to know and be confident that it pleases God for our households to be godly. It pleases Him for generations to be raised in an environment where He is Lord, trusted as the author and perfecter of our lives. Let the prayers below encourage you and galvanise your faith to intercede alongside Jesus to pray God's will for your family – whatever it looks and feel like now. Let God's Word inform your prayers.

Let Father manifest His desires through you, working through our communities one family at a time, starting with yours, starting with you. As you pray these prayers, I pray your household will be firmly under the banner of His protection, positioned to receive His provision, connected to feel His inspiration, alert to His instructions and responsive to His love, in Jesus name.

Prayers

Prayers for the Whole Family
- Anchor my family in the love of Jesus; regardless of what happens in life, ground us in the love of God.
- Holy Spirit, let our family be fully covered by God's banner of love, shielded from every attack of the enemy.
- I declare that nothing will separate my household from the love of God. God's love binds, keeps, protects and provides for us in Jesus name.
- Each member of my household will know the love of God, personally and intimately.
- God's love speaks for us, through us and over us.

Prayers and Declarations for our Men: Grace, Wisdom and Power
- I declare the men in my life to be Kingdom men – fathers, brothers, husbands, sons, nephews etc...
- I stand in the gap on their behalf and claim their souls for God's Kingdom. I partner with Jesus (Romans 8: 34) to intercede on their behalf that they discover and walk in their identity as sons of God, leaders, exemplary men, reputable and outstanding men of God.
- I scatter every demonic game plan playing out against the men in my life and in the Body of Christ.
- I declare that every demonic tactic concerning their

lives be exposed and destroyed now in the mighty name of Jesus.
- With the same power that resurrected Jesus from the dead, I call forth life, restoration, and redemption in the lives of the men in my life. I declare this is the acceptable time of the Lord for salvation. (2 Corinthians 6:2).

"And he will turn the hearts of fathers to their children and the hearts of children to their fathers..." (Malachi 4:6 ESV).

- Heavenly Father, help our fathers to lead by example when it comes to repentance and forgiveness. Help them have a humble disposition.
- Lord, cause our household to be led to a place of repentance, Holy Spirit turn our hearts to God.
- Turn the heart of fathers to their children. Touch their hearts to wake up to the call, and duty on them to lead as You would.
- Embolden and empower our fathers and the fathers of our children to firmly take up their role as high priests of the home. (Ephesians 5:21-23 NIV)

"For I have chosen him, that he may command his children and his household after him to keep the way of the Lord by doing righteousness and justice, so that the Lord may bring to Abraham what he has promised him." (Genesis 18:9 ESV).

- Let our men be led by Your Spirit, to live according to the calling of chosen ones to fulfil God's desire and plan within the family.
- Let our men lead exemplary lives, let them show the way to Christ, strengthen their bond and relationship

with Christ Jesus, so they are leading in all areas of their lives from a place of intimacy with God.
- I declare that our men are called and chosen of God to lead and live in holiness and righteousness.
- I declare that our men are the righteousness of God, and no plot of the enemy will circumvent that calling and mission in their lives in Jesus name. (2 Corinthians 5:21).

"Fathers, do not provoke your children to anger, but bring them up in the discipline and instruction of the Lord." (Ephesians 6:4 ESV).

- Holy Spirit, guide fathers in their parenting to fulfil their roles God's way, not the world's way.
- I break every worldly and demonic influence in the thoughts, actions of our men.
- I declare that every interaction, and decision they make will work out for good because they are called according to God's purpose. (Romans 8:28 NIV)

"And he arose and came to his father. But while he was still a long way off, his father saw him and felt compassion, and ran and embraced him and kissed him. And the son said to him, 'Father, I have sinned against heaven and before you. I am no longer worthy to be called your son.' But the father said to his servants, 'Quickly Bring the best robe, and put it on him, and put a ring on his hand, and shoes on his feet. And bring the fattened calf and kill it and let us eat and celebrate. For this my son was dead, and is alive again; he was lost, and is found.' And they began to celebrate." (Luke 15:20-24).

- Heavenly Father, I pray that our fathers will have a humble heart and live repentant lives yielded to Your

leadership.
- I pray they will be filled with the love, grace and mercy of God and overflow with the fruits of the Holy Spirit (Galatians 5:22)
- I pray Heavenly Father, that You would purge them of the desires of this world, the pride of life, lust of the eyes and the flesh and that they would be solely given to living a life that pleases You (1 John 2:16).
- Solidify their relationship with You, let them serve as high priests of the home from a place of relationship (not religion) with You in Jesus name.

"In the land of Uz there lived a man whose name was Job. This man was blameless and upright; he feared God and shunned evil... When a period of feasting had run its course, Job would make arrangements for them to be purified.

Early in the morning he would sacrifice a burnt offering for each of them, thinking, "Perhaps my children have sinned and cursed God in their hearts. This was Job's regular custom." (Job 1:1, 5 NIV).

- Raise our fathers to be intercessors, discerning, and committed to establishing a godly household always pleasing and acceptable in Your sight.
- Cleanse our home of worldliness invited in or that may have gained access inadvertently.
- Holy Spirit usher us to a place of collective and individual repentance as a household, that we are committed to living in holiness and godliness.
- Have mercy on us for those things we have done to displease or grieve the Holy Spirit, show us where we have gone wrong and restore us to a place of right standing with the Father.

"He established a testimony in Jacob and appointed a law in Israel, which he commanded our fathers to teach to their children, that the next generation might know them, the children yet unborn, and arise and tell them to their children, so that they should set their hope in God and not forget the works of God, but keep his commandments; and that they should not be like their fathers, a stubborn and rebellious generation, a generation whose heart was not steadfast, whose spirit was not faithful to God." (Psalm 78:5-8 ESV).

- As a household, help us, Holy Spirit, to be committed to righteous living.
- Establish us as a living testimony of God's faithfulness and goodness.
- Let our fathers echo the truth of our identity in Christ Jesus and establish a legacy of holiness and righteousness.
- Let our fathers respond diligently to the call on their lives to pass on the gospel from generation to generation.
- Lord God, break every generational curse on our lives in Jesus name.
- I declare that our fathers shall leave a legacy of the heritage of the righteous and not incur curses and punishment on our lineage (Psalm 37).

"And these words that I command you today shall be on your heart. You shall teach them diligently to your children, and shall talk of them when you sit in your house, and when you walk by the way, and when you lie down, and when you rise. You shall bind them as a sign on your hand, and they

shall be as frontlets between your eyes. You shall write them on the doorposts of your house and on your gates." (Deuteronomy 6:6-9).

- I declare that the Word of God shall not depart from my household.
- I declare that our hearts are fertile ground for God's word to grow and bring forth a bountiful harvest – generation after generation.
- I declare that our household is grounded in the word of God and our lives are established on the truth that is Jesus.
- Holy Spirit, fill us with a passion for the Word of God and bind it on our hearts and minds and grant us the grace to be diligent to live the truth of God's Word.

"...choose this day whom you will serve, whether the gods your fathers served in the region beyond the River, or the gods of the Amorites in whose land you dwell. But as for me and my house, we will serve the Lord." (Joshua 24:15 ESV).

- I declare that as for me and my household, we shall serve the Lord.
- Lord expose every form of idolatry in our household, usher us to a place of living repentant lives overcoming idolatry and everything contending to take Your place in our hearts.
- Holy Spirit, direct and guide our fathers to lead us in the service of our heavenly Father.
- Lord, I renounce every idol and false god in our lives in Jesus name.
- Lord Jesus, we pledge our allegiance to honour and uphold the will, plan, and purpose of God.

- Heavenly Father, we commit our lives to establishing your Kingdom here on earth and living lives driven by an eternity with You.

"Husbands, love your wives, as Christ loved the church and gave himself up for her, that he might sanctify her, having cleansed her by the washing of water with the word, so that he might present the church to himself in splendour, without spot or wrinkle or any such thing, that she might be holy and without blemish. In the same way husbands should love their wives as their own bodies. He who loves his wife loves himself. For no one ever hated his own flesh, but nourishes and cherishes it, just as Christ does the church..." (Ephesians 5:25-33 ESV).

- Father, let Your love dwell in us richly, let our household be founded on the love of Christ.
- Holy Spirit, help us to live our lives based on the truth of our identity as children of God, with humility and surrender to Christ Jesus.
- I pray the wisdom, grace, humility, and love of Christ overflows in the hearts of our fathers to serve and lead our households like Christ Jesus.
- Let love thrive and prosper in our household in Jesus name.
- Lord, heal the wounds of the past in the relationship between fathers and their children, between husbands and wives, and restore these relationships to a place of forgiveness, reconciliation, and love.
- Holy Spirit, let God's love restore and redeem our relationships especially when they may have been corrupted by sin and worldliness.
- Let our relationships be genuine, sincere and godly;

Lord Jesus be at the centre of our relationships.

Prayers and Declarations for Women:Identity, Grace and Love

There is more to a woman than the calling of wife and mother. God continues to raise godly women to defy the stereotypes of cultures and norms.

In Ephesians 6, Apostle Paul advises on family life within God's Kingdom. Verse after verse heralds the core message – be like Christ. Everyone within God's family must be committed to discovering their identity in Christ Jesus and living lives worthy of His calling on their lives.

Yes! Wives and mothers have a calling which, when seen from God's perspective, is powerful, crucial and pivotal to seeing His will and plan for His Kingdom fulfilled. Socio-cultural norms and rules have distorted this calling so much so, many women (families and communities) have been robbed of its blessing, the equipping and resources assigned to this amazing calling and, worst of all, cheated of the power and authority that comes with it. But no more!

Stepping into a deep and committed relationship with God is the eye-opening experience that seals our redemption. This intimacy reveals identity and purpose so whether married, single, divorced, or widowed, biological mother or not, God's gift and his call upon women are irrevocable (Romans 11:29).

When we consider ourselves from a godly perspective, we get closer to discovering and embracing who we are in Christ. When our eyes are focused on His perspective of who we are, nothing else will do.

Kingdom women all around the world are rising, discovering their identity as God's daughters and taking their place in His Kingdom. Within the family, God's Divine Enterprise, we see the powerful symbol of the Trinity as the embodiment of unity.

We're adopted into God's family when we receive the gift of salvation and through Christ Jesus, we can declare:

- The women in our lives are bold and courageous and have a powerful identity that comes from being adopted into God's Kingdom. They are valuable and influential in all God has assigned them to be as wives, mothers, entrepreneurs, professionals, leaders, creators, healers, and all the other areas of influence God has positioned them.
- Nothing and no one has the permission to rob the women in my life of the strength, grace and power bestowed on them by God through Christ Jesus.

"...He who began a good work in you will carry it on to completion until the day of Christ Jesus." (Phil 1:6).

- Lord give the women in my life vision and revelation of divine purpose and identity. Help them hear the instruction and direction for the life they've been called to live.
- Lord, I pray the women in my life will choose to partner with God's will and plan for the life He has called them to.
- Father, I trust that You will not allow anything to abort or destroy the work You have started in and through their lives. Holy Spirit, help them yield to You and step back from every form of self-sabotage obstructing your work in their lives.
- In the mighty name of Jesus, I destroy every effort to

sabotage God's work in their lives. I declare that every good work will be seen to completion in Jesus name.
- Holy Spirit, help our women walk in their identity as people who mirror God's image as creators, developers, nurturers, completers, and finishers because Christ is in them.

"Whatever happens, conduct yourself in a manner worthy of the gospel of Christ." (Phil 1:27).

- Holy Spirit, help the women in my life to be loyal to Christ Jesus, behind closed doors and on the world's stage. Let the very depth of their hearts be pleasing and acceptable in God's sight.
- Holy Spirit, help our women choose to release every area of their lives to You to lead, guide, and direct them in the path of holiness and righteousness.

As a woman I declare

- Jesus is the one who reigns supreme in my heart; everything I am about is to please and glorify Him.
- I claim victory over every attempt of the enemy to pull me out of the nature, mind and character of Christ. I declare that whatever happens, my actions, thoughts and words will reflect Christ Jesus in me.

"And this is my prayer; that your love may abound more and more in knowledge and depth of insight so that you may be able to discern what is best and may be pure and blameless for the day of Christ, filled with the fruit of righteousness that comes through Jesus Christ – to the glory and praise of God." (Phil 1:9)

Lord, as a woman:
- Help me grow in Your love; I receive the depth of insight to be discerning.

- Let my choices and decisions be based on the revelation and knowledge that comes from the Holy Spirit.
- Fill me with the fruit of righteousness, Lord.
- Purge me of worldliness and make me victorious over the manipulations and intimidation of the world.

"Direct me, Yahweh, throughout my journey so I can experience your plans for my life. Reveal the life-paths that are pleasing to you. Escort me into your truth; take me by the hand and teach me. For you are the God of my salvation; I have wrapped my heart into yours all day long!" (Psalm 25: 4-5 TPT)

- Lord, help our women trust You, direct and lead them through every process and season of life.
- Father, let our women fully experience your plans for their lives. Let it be for them as You intend.
- Father, align the lives of our women with Your heart's desires. For anyone living a narrative that You have not written, Father intervene, redeem, and restore to Your original plan and purpose.
- Expose every deception and falsehood, Father; dismantle every lie that confuses and distorts Your truth.
- Restore families, communities through Your restorative work in the lives of our women.
- Father, wrap our women up in You, secure their hearts in Yours throughout their lives.

Prayers and Declaration for Children: Destiny, Character, Purpose, and God's will

For those trusting God for a child

- Father, my heart longs for a child. Help me with this natural longing. Keep me within the parameters of Your love, Your word and Your will.
- Father, shield and guard my heart as I wait on You for a child. Let my heart be forever positioned in a place of hope, trust and faith. Let my confessions always be anchored on Your word.

"And hope does not put us to shame, because God's love has been poured out into our hearts through the Holy Spirit, who has been given to us." (Romans 5:5).

- I declare that I will not be put to shame as I hope in God.
- Lord, pour Your love into my heart in this season of waiting and trusting.
- Let my heart and my womb be filled with Your love so much so that even as I hope for the manifestation of this promise of life, I walk in faith and love.

"And by faith even Sarah, who was past childbearing age, was enabled to bear children because she considered him faithful who had made the promise." (Hebrews 11:11).

- I speak to my soul, have faith, trust God, and consider Him faithful to keep His promise.
- Father! I will praise You before I receive this breakthrough.

"Praise the Lord, my soul; all my inmost being, praise his holy name. Praise the Lord, my soul, and forget not all his benefits." (Psalm 103:1-2 NIV).

"As for me, I will always have hope; I will praise you more and more." (Psalm 71:14).

- Lord, this is where I want my heart to live, in a place where I'm praising You and hoping in Your promises.

- Heavenly Father, speak life into me. Fulfil this promise of a child.
- Lord, I pray for the grace to be the parent You need me to be for the child You have promised me.
- Lord, prepare our hearts and our home to raise this child on Your behalf.
- Lord, I pray that You parent this child through us. Help us share Your mind and heart concerning this child
- Lord, I thank You for this child.

For children of all ages

But the angel said to him, *"Do not be afraid, Zacharias, because your petition [in prayer] was heard, and your wife Elizabeth will bear you a son, and you will name him John. You will have great joy and delight, and many will rejoice over his birth, for he will be great and distinguished in the sight of the Lord; and will never drink wine or liquor, and he will be filled with and empowered to act by the Holy Spirit while still in his mother's womb. He will turn many of the sons of Israel back [from sin] to [love and serve] the Lord their God. It is he who will go as a forerunner before Him in the spirit and power of Elijah, to turn the hearts of the fathers back to the children, and the disobedient to the attitude of the righteous [which is to seek and submit to the will of God]—in order to make ready a people [perfectly] prepared [spiritually and morally] for the Lord."* (Luke 1:13-17 AMP)

- Lord, thank You for answered prayers concerning our children; thank You for blessing and trusting us with their lives.
- Lord, as You did to Elizabeth and Zechariah, speak to

us about who these children are, reveal the purpose for their lives, give us the instructions with which to raise them so they live their lives on Your terms and according to Your will.
- Holy Spirit, help us to be attentive and obedient to Father's instructions to raise these children.
- Lord, we choose to follow Your will for their lives.

"When her son was born, she named him Samson. And the Lord blessed him as he grew up. And the Spirit of the Lord began to stir him while he lived in Mahaneh-dan, which is located between the towns of Zorah and Eshtaol." (Judges 13:24-25 NLT).

God permitted His Spirit to stir the heart of young Samson. Destiny was brewing in Samson's heart. Father, I pray that You would:
- Bless our children, in all their endeavours, everywhere they go, let them be blessed. Let them find favour in your sight and in the sight of men.
- Father, let Your Spirit stir the hearts of each one of our children, right from the womb to the day they depart this earth; let Your Spirit stir them into being children of God and doing God's will.
- Father, if there be any evil deposits from the world on our children that incurs a curse, or that brings about demonic attacks, Jesus, I ask that the same resurrection power that raised Jesus from the grave would rise up and speak for them and break every curse, every stronghold, and destroy every scheme of the enemy against their lives (Romans 8:11).

Samson's parents were told the purpose of their son's life and the conditions and parameters within which he should be raised. Interestingly, breaking those very things brought about the defeat of the Philistines. Samson killed more Philistines in his death than in his lifetime. Jesus, I pray:

- Our children will be obedient to the leading to the Holy Spirit. That things would end well for them, that the purpose of their lives will be fulfilled. That every detail, every opportunity, hurt, betrayal, would work out for divine purpose in Jesus name.
- I pray for us, their parents, Father, that You would grant us revelation of who our children are and what they are called to be.
- Father, reveal the parameters within which our children should live their lives. Open our eyes to their identity, to see them as You do and to raise them as You would.
- Father, help us, teach us, and equip us to honour the call on our lives to parent them on Your behalf.
- Father, I pray for the grace, wisdom, and discernment to raise them in a godly way and help them discover and live out their identity as children of God. Help us never shrink back from this calling or treat it with disdain. Father, I offer myself as a vessel to be used by You in their lives.

"For I know the plans I have for you, declares the Lord, plans to prosper you and not to harm you, plans to give you hope and a future." (Jeremiah 29:11).

- I pray that regardless of their beginning, Lord, let our children arrive at the good end You have designed for them.
- I declare that our children will stand out from the crowd for good and that they will partner with heaven

for the fulfilment of divine purpose.

"At that time the Spirit of the Lord came upon Jephthah, and he went throughout the land of Gilead and Manasseh, including Mizpah in Gilead, and from there he led an army against the Ammonites." (Judges 11:29 NLT).

Jephthah went from hanging out with the wrong crowd to becoming a great leader who recruited an army, fought for a nation and won. Jesus, I pray for our children that:

- The Spirit of the Lord will come on them and do what only Jesus can do in their lives.
- I pray for their spiritual growth and maturity.
- Their circle of influence would be such that they surround themselves with those instrumental to the fulfilment of divine purpose, and the establishment of God's Kingdom here on earth.
- Lord, remove them from toxic, corrupt and destructive relationships outside of Your will for them. Unravel every plan and assignment of the enemy to infiltrate their lives through friendships, connections, acquaintances or affiliations.

Jephthah was good at rallying men together for a cause. He did so in the battle against the Ammonites and again when fighting against the men of Ephraim. Lord, I pray that:

- Our children will successfully rally people around the most important cause there this - establishing your Kingdom here on earth. Let them be instrumental in fulfilling your plan and purpose.

"He has showered his kindness on us, along with all wisdom and understanding." (Ephesians 1: 8 NLT).

- I declare that our children are leaders with wisdom, understanding and integrity, that they will take the time

to learn and grow in the things of the Lord.
- Father, thank You for pouring Your truth into their hearts let it reside there. Each child will be confident in the Truth and would not budge from it in Jesus name.

"No weapon formed against you shall prosper, and every tongue which rises against you in judgment you shall condemn. This is the heritage of the servants of the Lord, and their righteousness is from Me, Says the Lord." (Isaiah 54:17 NKJV).

- Jesus, I lift each child before you and trust that You are already laying the groundwork for the fulfilment of Your will in their lives. I believe You have already made a date and appointment with destiny for them.
- Jesus, I partner with You on interceding on their behalf that nothing will circumvent, prevent, corrupt Your plans for these children.
- I declare that every demonic tactic against their lives be destroyed; it will not work against them. I declare that in every realm, the path is clear for Kingdom purpose, plan and intent to prevail in their lives. I declare breakthrough, victory and success in every Kingdom strategy, tactic and activity concerning these children. I break every yoke of oppression, depression, and demonic possession over their lives in Jesus name.
- I declare our children are set apart for Kingdom purposes only and I confess my partnership with Jesus in making this happen. Jesus, here I am, speak to me, reveal to me my role in this, what to do and how to do it, and the resources to make this happen. Father, make it happen.

"I will lead them in paths they have not known. I will make

darkness light before them, And crooked places straight. These things I will do for them, and not forsake them." (Isaiah 42:16 NKJV).

"So do not fear, for I am with you; do not be dismayed, for I am your God. I will strengthen you and help you; I will uphold you with my righteous right hand." (Isaiah 41:10 NIV).

- Father, go ahead of our children, give them the boldness, wisdom and courage needed to be exceptional in business/career, marriage, their parenting and everything they do.
- Lord, I pray that they are guided by Your will in those everyday decisions that lead to the major life choices. Let them cultivate the trust and intimacy needed for a successful Kingdom life even now in their infancy/childhood/adolescence /youth.

"Your word is a lamp for my feet, a light to my path. I have taken an oath and confirmed it, that I will follow your righteous laws." (Psalm 119:105).

"The Lord makes firm the steps of the one who delights in him." (Psalm 37:23).

"Train up a child in the way he should go, and when he is old, he will not depart from it." (Proverbs 22:6 NJKV).

- Holy Spirit, lead our children to where they should be. I declare that our children will be well placed and positioned for favour, blessings, promotion and to receive everything Father has in store for them to accomplish what He has purposed and willed for their lives.
- Let our children be rooted in You, Father, as they are

brought up in the way they should go; I declare in the name of Jesus they will not depart from the path of life that pleases God.
- Father, an intimate relationship with You is a process; help us as parents to trust Your process for our children and to aid, not hinder it. Let the words of counsel, guidance, and leadership we speak over these children come from You.
- Lord, I speak Your promises of predestination, protection, goodness, favour and blessing over my children's future, over the people they will marry, those they will work with, those that will have influence over them. I declare that their lives will glorify You always in Jesus name.

I declare that it shall be well with them in Jesus name.

Section 3
Healing

For all our best intentions, poor health, be it emotional, psychological or physical, can take a toll on individual and family life.

So, within the Divine Enterprise, what is God's will for our bodies? Faith can easily get tested when it comes to wellness and health and there can be confusion about the connection between faith, sin and sickness. Many have tied themselves up in knots trying to understand why healing miracles performed by Jesus spoke to sin. Many others have had hopes dashed when prayers for healing have seemingly gone unanswered.

No two people are the same, but God is – now and always. We know and can trust that He is a loving Father and His love is enduring and everlasting. There is nothing we can do to make Him love us any more than He does now. In times of weakness and sickness, we can draw strength from knowing that God's love for us is complete.

As we ask for restoration in our physical being, let's open our hearts to the truth that He'll not only address symptoms, but also the very source of the ailment and its impact on us. When God heals, He heals completely in a way that we need, which may not always be what we ask for.

As we pray for healing, deliverance is released. To be

fully healed is to be set free. Many diseases are symptomatic of living in a fallen world; it's like planting a vine in toxic soil, over time it'll deteriorate. God the Master Vinedresser, when invited into our lives prunes us and transplants us in a lifestyle that nourishes our entire being – body, mind and soul. The healing and deliverance may be instant, for some it may be protracted, but when God does His thing, it is perfect. I pray we are all ready and willing to receive the full healing we need to not only survive but thrive in the life Father has called us to.

Prayers

Prayers and Declarations on Healing and Deliverance Faith, Forgiveness, and Life

"Have mercy on me, O Lord, for I am weak; O Lord, heal me, for my bones are troubled. My soul also is greatly troubled; But You, O Lord—how long? Return, O Lord, deliver me! Oh, save me for Your mercies' sake! For in death there is no remembrance of You; In the grave who will give You thanks?" (Psalm 6:2-5 NKJV).

- Father, I choose life! I declare that You alone have the power to restore health to my body. Father, have mercy on me and restore every part of my being, to perfect health.
- Everything is at Your disposal to restore me to perfect health; Father, I position myself to receive healing.

Shouts of joy and victory resound in the tents of the righteous: The Lord's right hand has done mighty things! The Lord's right hand is lifted high; the Lord's right hand has done mighty things! I will not die but live and will proclaim what the Lord has done." (Psalm 118: 15-17 NIV).

- Father, despite my current condition, fix my gaze on Your sovereignty, might, and goodness. Fix my gaze on the reality of who You are – a mighty God!
- Lord, I choose life. I declare that I will not die but live

to declare your greatness, Your might and goodness. Preserve my health to fulfil the length of days you have assigned to me.

"With a long life I will satisfy him and let him see My salvation." (Psalm 91:16 NKJ).

- Father, I claim salvation from every ailment, sickness or illness. I receive the long life You have intended for me. I declare wellness to my mind, body and soul for as long as I live.
- I declare I shall live in good health and strength to accomplish God's plan and purpose for my life.

"Jesus said to him, if you can believe, all things are possible to him who believes. Immediately the father of the child cried out and said with tears, Lord, I believe; help my unbelief! When Jesus saw that the people came running together, He rebuked the unclean spirit, saying to it, Deaf and dumb spirit, I command you, come out of him and enter him no more!" (Matthew 9:23-25 NKJV).

- If there be any unbelief or doubt in my heart, Lord, rid me of them. Holy Spirit, help me stand in a place of faith so that I receive the full and complete healing needed now.
- I know that all things, including full recovery, are possible with God because I believe in the healing power of Jesus.
- Thank You, Father, that in the name of Jesus I have the authority to renounce, cast out and rebuke sickness in my body. In Jesus name, I command sickness to come out of my body now in Jesus name.
- Jesus, cast out everything that is not of You in my life, in my body that has taken residence there.

- Lord, speak to my mind, body and soul and rebuke everything that's residing there against Your will.
- I declare that my body is the temple of the living God and will not host any opposing presence. I reject and renounce every spirit or presence that does not come from God now in the name of Jesus.
- I command every sickness and demonic power, presence and influence in my life and my body to be broken and destroyed now in Jesus name. I command them to get out now in Jesus name.
- I declare that I am well, I am whole, I am restored, I am redeemed in Jesus name.

"Praise the Lord, my soul; all my inmost being, praise his holy name. Praise the Lord, my soul, and forget not all his benefits—who forgives all your sins and heals all your diseases, who redeems your life from the pit and crowns you with love and compassion, who satisfies your desires with good things so that your youth is renewed like the eagle's." (Psalm 103:1-5 NIV).

- Holy Spirit, position my heart even now in a place of praise and worship. I command my body to perform in a way that gives God glory and praise.
- Father, I receive the forgiveness that leads to healing and restoration from anything that has brought a malfunction of my body, my mind and my soul.
- I receive the redemption that comes from God and I claim the fullness of life and peace that comes with God's love and compassion.
- I speak rejuvenation, healing and restoration to every part of my body in Jesus name.

"Worship the Lord your God, and his blessing will be on

your food and water. I will take away sickness from among you." (Exodus 23:25 NIV).
- Father, I worship You! I praise You and claim healing in every part of my body and deliverance from sickness and illness.
- I declare that sickness is removed from my household in Jesus name.
- Lord let my environment, food, water, nourish my life and bring strength and wellbeing to my body.

"Therefore, all those who devour you shall be devoured; And all your adversaries, every one of them, shall go into captivity; Those who plunder you shall become plunder, And all who prey upon you I will make a prey. For I will restore health to you and heal you of your wounds," says the Lord... (Jeremiah 30:17 NKJV).
- Every sickness that is an attack of the enemy is unacceptable! In Jesus name, I reject them.
- Every attack on my being must end now in Jesus name. Father, arise on my behalf and attack my attackers in Jesus name.
- I declare my health is restored; my wounds are healed in Jesus name!

Section 4
Business, Education, Finances

Ultimately each one of us within God's Kingdom has a call on our lives, and it serves us well to seek revelation on what God's plan and purpose is for our lives. The purpose of man is to please God. And it pleases God for man to be adopted into His family, co-heirs and co-workers with Christ Jesus in the eternal family business – God's Divine Enterprise. So each day is an opportunity to fulfil this revelation. We can be intentional with every thought, word and action to please God.

Living with an awareness of this truth positions us to be led and directed as beloved children of God. Pleasing and acceptable in His sight, discovering and operating in our divinely assigned roles, skills and with the talents and gifts we've been given. So, whatever we are doing in life – business, education, with our finances, we have the disposition to do so to please and honour God.

"Trust in the Lord completely, and do not rely on your own opinions. With all your heart rely on Him to guide you, and He will lead you in every decision you make.
Become intimate with Him in whatever you do, and He will lead you wherever you go." (Proverbs 4:5-6 TPT)

After an intense and fruitless season of striving in my own strength and knowledge to make things happen in my career, I , learned the hard way to surrender and adopt the advice of Proverbs 4:5-6. When I was prepared for Father to break the cycle of stress, frustration and discontent, I knew that the only way to start each day – as wife, mother, daughter, in ministry, finances and my career – was to let Jesus take the driving seat. I was prepared for Jesus to be all things for and through me.

Simply put, at work for instance, I'd resign my heart each day to the truth that Jesus works here [insert name of company, business]. Declaring this truth, shifted my perspective, mind and heart. Personal agenda and ambition seemed irrelevant; my mind inadvertently reverts to Christ to do what needs to be done. Can you imagine going to work every day knowing that Jesus is at work there through you?

Issues of capacity, questions of ability, threats of offense and temptation to get drawn into conflicts and disputes are resolved because Christ Himself is right at the heart of everything. This becomes increasingly real as I relinquish control to Him and choose to trust His will.

The work/life balance (rather imbalance) struggle somehow manages to find an equilibrium. Of course, there are days when everything around me challenges the truth of Christ in me, but in those moments of weakness, it's up to me to run to the Holy Spirit for the strength, focus and perspective I need to remain grounded.

God's Kingdom goals and plans for each life in the Divine Enterprise requires obedience. There is no shortage of choices that could easily lead us out of the will of God. It is critical that we are aware of our identity in Christ as we engage in this world and carefully choose to follow His way of life and choose to live life on His terms.

"But if God himself has taken up residence in your life, you

can hardly be thinking more of yourself than of him. Any one, of course, who has not welcomed this invisible but clearly present God, the Spirit of Christ, won't know what we're talking about. But for you who welcome him, in whom he dwells—even though you still experience all the limitations of sin—you yourself experience life on God's terms. It stands to reason, doesn't it, that if the alive-and-present God who raised Jesus from the dead moves into your life, he'll do the same thing in you that he did in Jesus, bringing you alive to himself? When God lives and breathes in you (and he does, as surely as he did in Jesus), you are delivered from that dead life. With his Spirit living in you, your body will be as alive as Christ's!" (Romans 8:9-11 MSG).

Kingdom citizens are in this world, but not of it, so the rules of engagement are different. Ambassadors of Christ – God's special operatives, live by Kingdom principles, not worldly ones. So engaging in the 'marketplace' means we need to remain aware of who we are and whose we are. To be alive in Christ, united with Him, sharing His mind and His heart is to live a successful life as defined by God.

I pray that as we engage with the prayers below, Father will pour out revelation in our hearts that will guide and direct us to fulfil purpose. I pray we are activated to represent Him and His Kingdom in all we do and that we excel in all our endeavours to His glory in Jesus name.

Prayers

Prayers over Education: Wisdom, Knowledge and Understanding

"To these four young men God gave knowledge and understanding of all kinds of literature and learning. And Daniel could understand visions and dreams of all kinds." (Daniel 1:17 NIV).

- Heavenly Father, grant me the aptitude for understanding all kinds of literature and learning to grow and expand my capacity to fulfil divine purpose and potential.
- I receive the grace and the anointing to excel academically and in all forms of training and learning in Jesus name.
- I have the mind of Christ; therefore, I am not overwhelmed by my studies. I can do all things through Christ who strengthens me (Philippians 4:13).
- Because I belong to Christ, I do not have the spirit of fear, but of power and a sound mind. I have a sound mind to process, analyse and retain information, draw knowledge from it and apply it wisely.
- The teaching and leading of the Holy Spirit will always cause me to excel in my education and in everything I do.
- The Lord is with me, and He causes everything I do to succeed, and I find favour. The favour of God brings me promotion, the favour of God causes me to excel in my education (Gen 39.8).

"For the LORD gives wisdom; from his mouth come knowledge and understanding." (Proverbs 2:6 NIV).
- Holy Spirit, refine my nature and character to be teachable, help me to patiently acquire wisdom, knowledge and understanding (Proverbs 4:5-9).
- Holy Spirit, help me to know how to understand information and know how to apply it in a way that yields great results.
- Lord, let the knowledge, wisdom and understanding that I gain be useful and applicable in a way that brings about a positive change and solution to the world around me.
- Lord, give me grace to use wisdom, knowledge and understanding from a disposition of love and humility (1 Cor 13:1 NIV).

"How much better to get wisdom than gold, to get insight rather than silver!" (Proverbs 16:16 NIV).

"The one who gets wisdom loves life; the one who cherishes understanding will soon prosper." (Proverbs 19:8).
- Lord, You see my heart, let my motives for learning always be right in Your sight.
- Regarding my academics and all forms of training and learning, help me be focused and set my priorities right.
- Lord, help me overcome every distraction when it comes to focusing on my learning; help me be diligent, and determined to succeed in all I do to study hard and smart.
- I declare that by God's grace I shall prosper in all my learning and academics in Jesus name. I shall excel.
- Lord, place in me the spirit of excellence to thrive and

to be outstanding in all my learning and academics in Jesus name.
- I shall be outstanding and excel in every exam, course work and every form of assessment, because the grace of God is on me for excellence.

Prayers and Declarations over Businesses/Careers: Mindset, Obedience, Provision

- The word of God says, 'as a man thinks so is he', (Proverbs:7) so I declare that I am rich, because Jesus Christ has made me rich. There is nothing I need that God has not already provided for me.
- I believe God and therefore I align myself and my mindset with His word. I cast down every thought, imagination and every stronghold trying to exalt itself against the true knowledge of God (Proverbs 23.7, 2 Corinthians 10:5).
- I declare that God is my provider. I always seek first His kingdom and His righteousness and everything I need, above and beyond is added onto me (Matt 6:33).
- I never lack any good thing, because God supplies all my needs according to His riches in glory by Christ Jesus (Phil. 4.19).
- I am the blessed of the Lord; I am blessed with God's blessing that makes rich with no sorrow added to it. I yield to God's word; therefore, I am blessed in every area of my life.
- I declare that the blessing of God goes into every area of my life restoring the abundance that God has supplied for me (Deuteronomy 28.1-13).

- I declare that the work of my hands is blessed, I always prosper in all that I set my hands to do, because God is the one that teaches my hands to prosper and teaches my hands to profit. (Isaiah 48.17, Deuteronomy 8.18, Deuteronomy 30.9)

"Look at the birds of the air; they do not sow or reap or store away in barns, and yet your heavenly Father feeds them. Are you not much more valuable than they? Can any one of you by worrying add a single hour to your life?" (Matthew 6: 26-27 NIV).

- Father, I thank You for making me abundantly prosperous in everything that I do, in my work and my business. Thank You Father, that because of Your Blessing, I am fruitful and productive in my career, my work, my business, in my investments; is blessed and overflowing. Thank You Lord for delighting in my prosperity (Deuteronomy 30.9, Psalm 35.27).
- I am a giver, I give generously to the things of God and to help others and as I do, God makes all grace abound towards me so that I always have an overflow with abundance in every good thing I do (Deuteronomy 15.10, 2 Corinthians 9:8).

"Now to him who is able to do immeasurably more than all we ask or imagine, according to his power that is at work within us, to him be glory in the church and in Christ Jesus throughout all generations, for ever and ever! Amen." (Ephesians 3:20 NIV).

- I choose to trust God's word and yield myself to His Blessing. I declare that God is my provider. God provides for me abundantly, beyond anything I can ever imagine. I am willing and obedient to God; therefore, I always eat the good of the land. I am blessed (Matthew 6:26-27, Isaiah 1:19, Ephesians 3:20).

- According to the word of God, a good man leaves an inheritance for his children's children (Proverbs 13:22). I declare that I am good, and I will leave a wealthy inheritance for my children and children's children.

The Lord is my shepherd; He supplies all my needs. He makes me lie down in green pastures, abundant blessing and provision. I never lack anything. The Lord always causes my supply, my provision to overflow with abundance (Psalm 23:1-2, 6).

- Lord, I ask for the wisdom to prosper. I ask for the wisdom to make right decisions and be able to hear You when you are giving me instructions. I declare that I recognise Your voice, Lord, and I will obey You.

"If any of you lacks wisdom [to guide him through a decision or circumstance], he is to ask of [our benevolent] God, who gives to everyone generously and without rebuke or blame, and it will be given to him. But he must ask [for wisdom] in faith, without doubting [God's willingness to help], for the one who doubts is like a billowing surge of the sea that is blown about and tossed by the wind. For such a person ought not to think or expect that he will receive anything [at all] from the Lord, being a double-minded man, unstable and restless in all his ways [in everything he thinks, feels, or decides]" (James 1:5-8 AMP).

- I am led by the Spirit of God; therefore, I am a son of God (Romans 8.14).
- I yield myself to God's wisdom; therefore, I am like the steward who knew how to multiply his master's

money. I am a good steward of all that God has entrusted me with and by the leading of the Holy Spirit, I make the right decisions on how to make money, how to invest money, how to multiply money; I make money work for me and not I for money, because I only serve one master and that is God (1 Corinthians 1.30).

- I am not shaken when things look difficult, because I know that my Father is my source and my provider; He owns the cattle on a thousand hills, everything on the earth belongs to Him, resource was made by and for Him.

"By wisdom a house is built, and through understanding it is established; through knowledge its rooms are filled with rare and beautiful treasures." (Proverbs 24:3-4 NIV).

- I declare that Jesus has been made wisdom onto me and through wisdom my house is built, and by understanding my house is established. The Holy Spirit gives me knowledge and by this knowledge my rooms are filled with all precious and pleasant riches (1 Corinthians 1.30).
- Father, I pray that You will cause me to be aligned in my work, job, choice of career, business. May I be aligned with Your will, Your plan and Your purposes for me. Help me to yield completely to You.
- Thank You for the opportunities that You provide for me daily. Thank You Lord that I never miss the opportunities You provide and that I have everything I need to take good advantage of them. Thank You for blessing me with excellent gifts and talents.

"To the person who pleases him, God gives wisdom, knowledge, and happiness, but to the sinner he gives the task of gathering and storing up wealth to hand it over to

the one who pleases God. This too is meaningless, a chasing after the wind." (Ecclesiastes 2:26 NIV).

Thank You Father, for calling me into business. I thank You for blessing my business and the work of my hand. May my business be a success and produce abundantly, to Your glory. I pray that my business will grow and develop so that I am able to leave it as an inheritance for future generations to come (Psalm 90:16-17, Proverbs 13:22).

- Lord, I pray that You would prosper the work of my hands (Psalm 90:16-17).
- Father, I thank you for Your word. I have declared according to Your word; therefore, I fully expect the manifestation of Your blessing in my life, because Your word never returns to You void; it always accomplishes what You have sent it to do (Isaiah 55:10-12).
- Lord your word never fails, it stands forever (1 Peter 1:25). Thank You, because I can trust that Your word concerning me will be accomplished abundantly in my life.
- The blessing of the Lord has made me rich and has added no sorrow (Proverbs 10:22).
- I always find favour in my finances because the favour of God surrounds me as a shield; it always goes before me to prepare a way for me.
- Lord, I ask You for the wisdom to be a good steward of the resources You have placed in my hands and in my life. Teach me to steward what You have given me in a way that is pleasing to You (James 1:5).
- The Lord is with me and He causes everything I do to succeed and I find favour. The favour of God brings me promotion; the favour of God causes me to excel in my

work/business (Genesis 39:8).
- I trust in the Lord; therefore, I am like a tree planted by water, that sends out its roots by the stream, and does not fear when heat comes, for my leaves remain green, and I am not anxious in the year of drought, for I never cease to bear fruit (Jeremiah 17:7-8).

Prayers and Declarations over Finances: Faith, Humility, Trust

"For you know the grace of our Lord Jesus Christ, that though he was rich, yet for your sake he became poor, so that you through his poverty might become rich." (2 Corinthians 8:9 NIV).

- Father, in the name of Jesus, I thank You that I have been made a new creation, behold, old things have passed away and I have become new.
- By faith I take hold of my new identity in Christ, breaking any attachments with generational curses and mindsets, and I claim the riches Jesus Christ bought for me, by taking my poverty and giving me His riches.
- I declare boldly that I am rich.

"No one can serve two masters. Either you will hate the one and love the other, or you will be devoted to the one and despise the other. You cannot serve both God and money." (Matthew 6:24 NIV).

- Holy Spirit, help me to unlearn and renounce all the lies and deceptions regarding money.
- Holy Spirit, release me from the hold and power of money, lead me to a place where I am truly serving God and not mastered by money or the lack of money.
- I choose to trust God with my needs, wants and desires; Holy Spirit, let everything be aligned with

God's will, plan, purpose and provision.
- Heavenly Father, thank You because You love me and You meet every need.

"You may say to yourself, *my power and the strength of my hands have produced this wealth for me. But remember the Lord your God, for it is he who gives you the ability to produce wealth.*" (Deuteronomy 8:18 NIV).

- Holy Spirit, help me to receive the ability, wisdom and capacity to make wealth.
- Heavenly Father, help me to create things and offer services that deliver value and glorify You.
- Holy Spirit, help me to seek after God and not money and to discover my purpose, my abilities and to operate under the favour of God to be prosperous.

"Cast your cares on the Lord and he will sustain you; he will never let the righteous be shaken." (Psalm 55:22 NIV).

"Humble yourselves, therefore, under God's mighty hand, that he may lift you up in due time. Cast all your anxiety on him because he cares for you." (1 Peter 5:6 NIV).

"Keep your lives free from the love of money and be content with what you have, because God has said, "Never will I leave you; never will I forsake you." So, we say with confidence, "The Lord is my helper; I will not be afraid. What can mere mortals do to me?" (Hebrews 13:5-6 NIV).

- I cast every fear, worry and anxiety about my finances and resources on to Jesus.
- Lord, I bring to You my career, business, income, savings, every bill, every financial commitment, and I ask for Your intervention, provision, and solution.

- I declare that I trust the Lord to meet my needs today and every day. and I receive the wisdom to walk in financial freedom and prosperity.

"The earth is the LORD's, and everything in it. The world and all its people belong to him." (Psalm 24:1 NLT).

"Yours, Lord, is the greatness and the power and the glory and the majesty and the splendour, for everything in heaven and earth is yours. Yours, Lord, is the kingdom; you are exalted as head over all. Wealth and honour come from you; you are the ruler of all things… Everything comes from you, and we have given you only what comes from your hand." (1 Chronicles 29:10-12, 14 NIV).

- Holy Spirit, help me to be free and generous with what You have entrusted to me.
- Heavenly Father, thank You because everything that comes to me is from You; open my eyes, my heart and my ears to use the resources as directed by You and as pleasing to You.
- Rule over my finances Lord, take charge and control of it, release Kingdom resources to me and the wisdom to administer and steward it.

Section 5
Sound Mental Health

We wrestle with thoughts, emotions, and feelings that we do not always understand. We find ourselves in circumstances that impact and have a ripple effect on those around us. One healthy mind could significantly impact the disposition of another, and likewise, a broken mind could infect the countenance of those around us.

The Divine Enterprise is structured as a place of growth, nurturing and healing. It's also the first place where hurt, resentment and brokenness are experienced. What is God's heart for us within the family to experience and foster mental, emotional and spiritual wellness? As children of God, we have a choice to reject psychological victimisation. Let's be aware of our identity, power, authority and control – not just in theory, but in practice, in our physical, mental, psychological and emotional wellbeing.

People perish due to a lack of knowledge of who God says they are and what He has given access to. Going through scripture, we discover that God equips his children with every resource to overcome every challenge. Those moments of weakness are the most opportune times to delve into the Word of God and draw grace and strength to overcome every battle for our hearts and minds.

Declaring Identity
- Because I have received Christ Jesus and I believe in

His name, I have the right to be a child of God. I declare that I am a child of God and no one can take this away from me (John1:12).
- God predestined me to be adopted as His child through Jesus and this pleases Him, so I claim my sonship to the King of Kings! (Ephesians 1:5).
- Christ has accepted me, though the world rejects or ridicules me, I am loved by God and accepted by Jesus, this is enough for me (Romans 15:7).
- I have been brought to fullness in Christ Jesus who is the head over every power and authority. I am enough just as I am because Christ makes me whole and complete (Colossians 2:9-10).
- I am one with Christ Jesus because His Spirit resides in me so everything outside of God has no power, influence, or authority over me (1 Corinthians 6:17).
- I am created in the image of God, I am fearfully and wonderfully made, everything about me is perfect (Genesis 1:27, Psalm 139:14).
- I am chosen to be part of God's Kingdom; this means I am part of a royal lineage of priests and leaders, God's special one created to declare His praises (1 Peter 2:9).
- I have been called by God, through Jesus, out of darkness into God's wonderful light, everything about me radiates God's goodness and glory (1 Peter 2:9).
- No man can determine my worth. I am valuable and of great worth. I am not my own. God paid the ultimate price to secure my life, salvation, and redemption (1 Corinthians 6:19-20).
- I am loved by God. He lavishes His love on me and does not hold back from loving me. There is nothing I can do to make Him love me more or less. His love for

me is whole and complete (1 John 3:1-2).
- Situations and circumstances of this world will not bring me down because I have been raised with Christ! I choose to set my mind on things above because my life is hidden with Christ in God! (Colossians 3:1-3)

Prayers
"Create a clean heart for me, God; put a new, faithful spirit deep inside me!" (Psalm 51:10 CEB).
- Lord, purge my heart, mind and thoughts of those things not of You, purify my heart and birth in me a spirit that is faithful to You, let my thoughts, feelings and actions never betray You.
- I declare that every thought, every feeling, every emotion be aligned to God Most High.
- I declare that my heart is fully and deeply God's, and I will be faithful and loyal to Him alone.
- I command my thoughts and feelings to align with the Spirit of God now in Jesus name.

"Finally, brothers, whatever is true, whatever is honourable, whatever is just, whatever is pure, whatever is lovely, whatever is commendable, if there is any excellence, if there is anything worthy of praise, think about these things." (Philippians 4:8 ESV).
- Holy Spirit, help me to fix my thoughts on only the things that meet Your approval.
- Holy Spirit give me the strength to turn away from those toxic thoughts that pollute and corrupt my heart and my mind.
- I declare that my life is founded on what is good, true, honourable, just, pure, lovely and of good report.
- I command my soul to fixate on only what is

praiseworthy. I reject every negative, deceptive, anxious thought and take on every good, pleasant, true and praiseworthy truth from the Holy Spirit.

"For God hath not given us the spirit of fear; but of power, and of love, and of a sound mind." (2 Timothy 1:7 KJV).

- I reject fear in the name of Jesus; I claim the power, love and the sound mind made available to me through Christ Jesus.
- I declare that I am powerful, I have self-control and self-discipline and a sound mind, I am not afraid of anyone or anything.
- I declare that I'm walking in power and authority given to me through Christ Jesus.

"When hard pressed, I cried to the Lord; he brought me into a spacious place. The Lord is with me; I will not be afraid. What can mere mortals do to me? The Lord is with me; he is my helper. I look in triumph on my enemies." (Psalm 118:5-7 NIV).

- I step into the safe and spacious place provided by God. I am protected and covered mentally and spiritually in Jesus name.
- Thank You, Lord, for always being with me. I am not alone; I have nothing to fear.
- I declare no man has more power over me than Christ Jesus. I declare that only the will, plan and purpose of God shall prevail over my life in Jesus name.
- I have nothing to fear because the Lord is with me; He is my helper and I shall look with triumph on everyone who operates contrary to His will for my life in Jesus name!

"Do not be conformed to this world, but be transformed by

the renewal of your mind, that by testing you may discern what is the will of God, what is good and acceptable and perfect." (Romans 12:2 ESV).

- I declare that I am a citizen of God's Kingdom, my mind and perspective are transformed and aligned to Kingdom perspective and principles.
- I renounce world thinking and declare my allegiance with the Kingdom of God.
- Heavenly Father, give me Kingdom perspectives of the world and society I am in, let me see life through Your eyes and operate under divine wisdom.
- Holy Spirit, help me to always discern what is the will of God and to respond to this discernment with wisdom and obedience.

"We destroy arguments and every lofty opinion raised against the knowledge of God, and take every thought captive to obey Christ." (2 Corinthians 10:5 ESV).

- Holy Spirit, help me to live in obedience one instruction at a time so that my obedience may always be complete.
- I pull down and destroy everything that raises itself against the knowledge of God concerning my life, my household, ministry, finances and career in Jesus name.
- I command everything that opposes Christ in my life to be obedient to Christ Jesus in my life.

"And he said, what comes out of a person is what defiles him. For from within, out of the heart of man, come evil thoughts, sexual immorality, theft, murder, adultery, coveting, wickedness, deceit, sensuality, envy, slander, pride, foolishness." (Mark 7:20-22 ESV).

"The tongue can bring death or life; those who love to talk will reap the consequences." (Proverbs 18:21 NLT).
- Holy Spirit, let everything that comes out of my mouth come from a place of purity.
- Holy Spirit, help me to speak words that build up and not tear down, that declare light, life, hope and peace.
- I speak life over my family, my ministry, career, finances, and everything I have been called to in Jesus name.

"Therefore, preparing your minds for action, and being sober-minded, set your hope fully on the grace that will be brought to you at the revelation of Jesus Christ." (1 Peter 1:13 ESV).
- Holy Spirit, prepare my mind for action, help me to be sober-minded and set my hopes and expectations on Christ Jesus.
- I reject every addictive, corrosive thing that would weaken my mind and corrupt my thoughts.
- Holy Spirit, help me to fix my heart on things that are pleasing and acceptable to the Lord.
- I renounce evil desires and pursuits and align my heart and thoughts with the Holy Spirit.

"Submit yourselves therefore to God. Resist the devil, and he will flee from you." (James 4:7 ESV).
- Holy Spirit, give me the grace and the strength to resist the devil and to push back on every temptation that comes my way.
- I submit myself to the Lord, my heart, my thoughts, my words and my actions.
- Satan, I command you to get behind me; you have been defeated by Christ Jesus who has overcome the world, so I am victorious in Christ Jesus.

"For those who live according to the flesh set their minds on the things of the flesh, but those who live according to the Spirit set their minds on the things of the Spirit. For to set the mind on the flesh is death, but to set the mind on the Spirit is life and peace. For the mind that is set on the flesh is hostile to God, for it does not submit to God's law; indeed, it cannot." (Romans 8:5-7 ESV).

- I actively detach my thoughts from the world view and perspectives impressed on me. I intentionally seek God's view and perspective on life and set my mind on the things of God's Spirit.
- I choose to live according to the Spirit of God and as a result I live a victorious life as God's child seated with Jesus in heavenly places (Ephesians 2:6).
- I receive the revelation available to me through God's Spirit, I actively seek God's opinion, thoughts and mindset regarding my circumstances and the world around me.
- I claim the life and peace that comes with setting my mind on the things of the Spirit.

"But the wisdom from above is first pure, then peaceable, gentle, open to reason, full of mercy and good fruits, impartial and sincere." (James 3:17 ESV).

- Lord, I pray that You will position me like a tree planted by the rivers to steadily receive wisdom from above.
- Holy Spirit, let my heart be filled with the love of God that ensures that I am responsible and accountable for divine wisdom.
- Holy Spirit, I trust that by Your grace, divine wisdom will bear good fruit in my life.

Lord, I thank you!

Take time out to thank God for personal victories. Praise God sincerely for the boldness and confidence He has invested in you. Trust that God is a good Father and it is part of His good plan that you live up to the power and authority He has given you.

Access has been granted to you to exert divine influence in every sphere of your life; praise God for this, thank Him for it. Ask the Holy Spirit to guide you step by step as you receive all that has been apportioned for you.

Declarations of Power and Authority
I declare that…

- I am from God and greater is He who is in me than he who is in the world!

"Little children, you are from God and have overcome them, for he who is in you is greater than he who is in the world." (1 John 4:4 ESV).

- Signs and wonders will follow me because I believe in Christ Jesus. In His name I have the power and authority to cast out demons and speak truth and power to the effect of breakthrough, deliverance, edification and liberty.

"And these signs will accompany those who believe: in my name they will cast out demons; they will speak in new tongues." (Mark 16:17 ESV).

- God has given me full authority to trample on everything that opposes His original plan and design. I have authority over all the power of the enemy, and nothing shall by any means hurt me.

"Behold, I have given you authority to tread on serpents and scorpions, and over all the power of the enemy, and nothing shall hurt you." (Luke 10:19 ESV).

- Because all authority has been given to Jesus and He resides, I am a coheir of this authority, and wield it unhindered and unapologetically to establish God's Kingdom here on earth.

"Then Jesus came to them and said, all authority in heaven and on earth has been given to me. Go therefore and make disciples of all the nations, baptising them in the name of the Father and of the Son and of the Holy Spirit, teaching them to observe all things that I have commanded you; and lo, I am with you always, even to the end of the age." (Matthew 28: 18-20 NIV).

- I have been equipped and resourced with mighty weapons to pull down strongholds, cast down arguments and everything that exalts itself against the knowledge of God.
- I have the authority to take captive everything that exalts and opposes the knowledge of God.

"For though we walk in the flesh, we do not war according to the flesh. For the weapons of our warfare are not carnal but mighty in God for pulling down strongholds, casting down arguments and every high thing that exalts itself against the knowledge of God, bringing every thought into captivity to the obedience of Christ." (2 Corinthians 10:3-5).

- My life is backed by the power and authority that comes from being in God's presence and being God's child.

"What then shall we say to these things? If God is for us, who can be against us?" (Romans 8:31).

- I am more than a conqueror through Christ who loves me. Nothing can separate me from this love; as a result, I claim power and authority over everything that attempts to do so.

"Who shall separate us from the love of Christ? Shall tribulation, or distress, or persecution, or famine, or nakedness, or peril, or sword? As it is written: For Your sake we are killed all day long; we are accounted as sheep for the slaughter. Yet in all these things we are more than conquerors through Him who loved us. For I am persuaded that neither death nor life, nor angels nor principalities nor powers, nor things present nor things to come, nor height nor depth, nor any other created thing, shall be able to separate us from the love of God which is in Christ Jesus our Lord." (Romans 8:35-39).

- God has delivered me from the power of darkness and translated me into His Kingdom! I am redeemed from death and sin through the blood of Jesus.

"... strengthened with all might, according to His glorious power, for all patience and longsuffering with joy; giving thanks to the Father who has qualified us to be partakers of the inheritance of the saints in the light. He has delivered us from the power of darkness and conveyed us into the kingdom of the Son of His love in whom we have redemption through His blood, the forgiveness of sins. "(Colossians 1:11-14).

- I am authorised to take dominion, to lead, rule and multiply; I renounce everything that is contrary to this in my life in Jesus name.

"God blessed them; and God said to them, Be fruitful and multiply, and fill the earth, and subdue it; and rule over the fish of the sea and over the birds of the sky and over every living thing that moves on the earth." (Genesis 1:28).

Declarations and Prayers for Overcoming Fear
"Tell everyone who is discouraged, Be strong and don't be afraid! God is coming to your rescue..." (Isaiah 35:4 GNT).

In so many ways this is the Good News right at the heart of humanity's story as told by God. Reading the Bible from cover to cover, we know that's really God's heart for people, to know that He loves us and created us to be in relationship with Him. When fear, anxiety and worry set in, it is easy to forget this truth that God is sovereign and omniscient, His all-encompassing love has the capacity to save, restore and redeem us. As you read and pray through the scriptures below, be reminded that God is greater than any source of fear, be encouraged to know that God is coming to your rescue to deliver and save so we need not fear anything or anyone.

"For God did not give us a spirit of timidity or cowardice or fear, but [He has given us a spirit] of power and of love and of sound judgment and personal discipline [abilities that result in a calm, well-balanced mind and self-control]. (Timothy 1:7 AMP)

- I reject and rebuke the spirit of fear, cowardice and timidity in Jesus name. I part ways with it from today and refuse to permit it to operate in my life.
- I receive God's Spirit of love, sound judgement and personal discipline and choose to respond to His leading in every thought and action.
- I choose to operate in the abilities that lead to a calm, well-balanced mindset and yield to the leading, grace and strength of the Holy Spirit to operate in self-control.

Overcoming Fear of People

"Stir into flame the strength and boldness that is in you, that entered into you when I laid my hands upon your head and blessed you. For the Holy Spirit, God's gift does not want you to be afraid of people, but to be wise and strong, and to love them and enjoy being with them." (1 Timothy 1:6-7 Living Bible).

- Father, You make me bold and brave, Your Spirit in me transforms my weakness; lay Your hand on me, Lord, and let me be courageous.
- Holy Spirit, give me the wisdom and confidence I need to be fearless.
- Holy Spirit, give me a 'God perspective' of people, let His love for them and His heart towards them inform my disposition towards them.
- Lord, help me to enjoy being in community with others, help me choose the right response to the world around me such that I respond with boldness, strength and love.

"I tell you, my friends, do not be afraid of those who kill the body and after that can do no more. But I will show you whom you should fear: Fear him who, after your body has been killed, has authority to throw you into hell. Yes, I tell you, fear him." (Luke 12:4-5).

Lord, minister to my heart the truth about who I am, let your words embolden me.

- Lord, my mind may never fully comprehend Your greatness, but help me to grasp enough to live in awe and reverence of who You are.
- Holy Spirit, instil in me the fear of God.

- I renounce the fear of man over God, I renounce the fear of man.

"The Lord is my light and my salvation—Whom shall I fear? The Lord is the refuge and fortress of my life—Whom shall I dread? When the wicked came against me to eat up my flesh, My adversaries and my enemies, they stumbled and fell." (Psalm 27:1).

- I choose to fear the Lord; Holy Spirit guide my heart in the path that honours and reveres God, so that this positions my thoughts, feelings and actions (Proverbs 9:10 NIV).
- What God thinks is of paramount importance to me, it supersedes what man thinks or expects of me.
- My life will not be governed or influenced by the fear of man.
- I rebuke every attempt/ attack/act of intimidation aimed at me and I stand in the power and authority given to me by God through Christ Jesus.
- I establish as fact that because of God in me, every adversary that rises up against me shall fall and I will not be afraid, I will not be shaken in Jesus name.

"For I am the Lord your God who takes hold of your right hand and says to you, do not fear I will help you." (Isaiah 41:13).

"I sought the Lord, and he answered me, he delivered me from all my fears. Those who look to him are radiant; their faces are never covered with shame. This poor man called, and the Lord heard him; he saved him out of all his troubles. The angel of the Lord encamps around those who fear him, and he delivers them." (Psalm 34:4-7 NIV).

- Lord, I confess my fears to You and I look to You for

strength, boldness and confidence; let me not be put to shame, give me the courage to face those who intimidate me.
- Lord, lead me, guide me and speak through me as I face those who stand against me and make me feel fearful; help me Lord to stand tall and bold.
- I destroy every work of manipulation and intimidation and every campaign set out against me and declare that no weapon formed against me shall prosper and every accusing tongue that rises against me in judgement shall fall in Jesus name (Isaiah 54:17 KJV).

Overcoming Fear of the Unknown

"Even though I walk through the darkest valley, I will fear no evil, for you are with me; your rod and your staff, they comfort me." (Psalm 23:4 NIV).
- Lord, I choose to rest in the comfort of Your presence, regardless of what lies ahead, because You are with me, I will not be fearful.
- Lord Jesus go ahead of me, let Your hand of protection rest on me to keep me safe from all harm.
- Holy Spirit, help me to stay in the path the Lord has laid for me that I do not go astray or miss my way.

"He will cover you with his feathers, and under his wings you will find refuge; his faithfulness will be your shield and rampart. You will not fear the terror of night, nor the arrow that flies by day, nor the pestilence that stalks in the darkness, nor the plague that destroys at midday. A thousand may fall at your side, ten thousand at your right hand, but it will not come near you. You will only observe with your eyes and see the punishment of the wicked." (Psalm 91:4-8 NIV).

- I declare that I am God's child, and I am under His protection.
- Thank You Father for your faithfulness; I declare that everything concerning me falls under the jurisdiction of God's Kingdom and he defends and protects me from all harm and every attack of the enemy; I have nothing to fear.
- I declare that I am not afraid of anything, be it in the day, or night, in the physical or spiritual because I am firmly under the protection of the Almighty God.
- No harm will come near me in Jesus name, I am safe and blessed in my going out and coming in, no weapon formed against me shall prosper and every accusing tongue that rises against me in judgement shall fall in Jesus name.

"Therefore, do not worry about tomorrow, for tomorrow will worry about itself. Each day has enough trouble of its own." (Matthew 6:34).

- Lord, I choose Your plan and will for my life and I declare that I trust You.
- I will not be afraid of what lies ahead; I declare that my tomorrow is in God's hands, and He will provide all my needs according to His riches in glory and keep me safe and secure.
- Regardless of what is happening around me, I choose to trust the Lord has a good tomorrow in store for me.

"There is no fear in love. But perfect love drives out fear, because fear has to do with punishment. The one who fears is not made perfect in love." (1 John 4:18 NIV).

- I am loved by God and the love of God dwells in me, so I declare that there is no room for fear in my life.

- I declare that I have the capacity to love others and have no cause to fear nor be intimidated.
- I am safeguarded by the perfect love of God and because it resides in me, I command fear to depart from my life in Jesus name.

Overcoming Fear of Circumstances and Challenges

"Then the Lord said to Joshua, Do not be afraid; do not be discouraged. Take the whole army with you and go up and attack Ai. For I have delivered into your hands the king of Ai, his people, his city and his land. You shall do to Ai and its king as you did to Jericho and its king, except that you may carry off their plunder and livestock for yourselves. Set an ambush behind the city." (Joshua 8:1 NIV).

- Holy Spirit, regardless of how fearful the situation is, help me to listen for Your guidance and instruction.
- Lord God, I receive deliverance from every problem, challenge and difficulty that lies ahead.
- I declare that I will succeed and emerge victorious from every challenge that lies ahead because the Lord is with me.
- I will not be afraid of the opposition and adversaries in my life because Almighty God is my God and he strengthens me and will help. Thank You Father, because You will uphold me with Your righteous right hand." (Isaiah 41:10 NJKV).

Section 6
Aligning with God's Agenda

God has made promise after promise to His family; they can be found in the Bible and are continually revealed to those in intimate relationship with The Trinity. Upon close study we see that God's blessings, gifts and call on our lives have a broader purpose beyond our lives. In fact, God's gaze is fixed on the 'apple of His eye', the Bride of Christ, the Church – the whole family of God.

Reading through the Old Testament and through to the New, we see that each child of God is created to thrive within the Ekklesia, which is God's Kingdom here on earth. God's love as expressed through His favour and blessing manifests and multiplies when we are adopted into His family.

To pray for the Body of Christ is to connect with the Father's heart for it, and effectively for ourselves, our success, our victory, our breakthrough – as one family. We are victorious together. Each child of God has a duty and responsibility to seek the Lord on behalf of the Church. Below are scripture-based prayers to guide and encourage prayers with a focus on when you worship and for the Church as a whole.

Prayers for the Body of Christ: Unity, Love, and the Father's Heart
"Even before he made the world, God loved us and chose us in Christ to be holy and without fault in his eyes. God

decided in advance to adopt us into his own family by bringing us to himself through Jesus Christ. This is what he wanted to do, and it gave him great pleasure. So we praise God for the glorious grace he has poured out on us who belong to his dear Son. He is so rich in kindness and grace that he purchased our freedom with the blood of his Son and forgave our sins. He has showered his kindness on us, along with all wisdom and understanding." (Ephesians 1:4-8 NLT).

- Father, it pleases you to have us in your family! What great news! Lord, help us the Body of Christ, to respond to this great invitation of love and identity every day with a sincere, 'Yes'.
- Father, I thank You for Your grace upon the believers at [name of Church]. Help us to walk in the forgiveness, power, identity and deliverance that comes with this grace.
- Thank You because your grace has set us free from sin and death. Thank You for showering us with kindness.
- Holy Spirit, help us to walk in the divine wisdom and understanding that God has given us through Jesus.

"And pray in the Spirit on all occasions with all kinds of prayers and requests. With this in mind, be alert and always keep on praying for all the Lord's people. Pray also for me, that whenever I speak, words may be given me so that I will fearlessly make known the mystery of the gospel." (Ephesians 6:17-19 NIV).

Just after listing the full armour of God, Apostle Paul encourages believers to be perpetual and consistent in praying for fellow believers – members of God's family. We have a responsibility to spend our faith on the things that matter to God, and the Body of Christ is His priority. Below are scripture-based prayers to guide and encourage us to stand alongside Jesus as He intercedes for The Church – His Bride.

"I will remain in the world no longer, but they are still in the world, and I am coming to you. Holy Father, protect them by the power of your name, the name you gave me, so that they may be one as we are one." (John 17:11 NIV).

- Lord, I pray for unity in the Spirit for the Body of Christ as expressed where I worship. I pray for a oneness of heart and mind.
- Father, let Your family, be submitted to Your Spirit not just in word, but in deeds. Holy Spirit lead us, guide us and keep us under the leadership of Christ Jesus.
- Jesus, You are the head of this body… help us to be focused on You, to share Your heart, perspective, and passions. Holy Spirit help us to truly be an expression of Christ where You have planted us. Let those around us see and experience You through us.

"Abide in Me, and I in you. As the branch cannot bear fruit of itself, unless it abides in the vine, neither can you, unless you abide in Me. I am the vine, you are the branches. He who abides in Me, and I in him, bears much fruit; for without Me you can do nothing." (John 15: 4-5 NKJV).

- Father, no matter what the world throws our way, help us to be rooted in You.
- Father, thank You because in you we will be fruitful and productive in all You have called us to do.
- Holy Spirit, help us to abide in the Lord at all times and to live lives that glorify God (1Corinthians 10:31).

- Lord, bring eternal results out of our time-bound efforts. Reveal to us the Kingdom strategies that will establish Your will and fulfil Your purpose.

"Whatever happens, conduct yourselves in a manner worthy of the gospel of Christ. Then, whether I come and see you or only hear about you in my absence, I will know that you stand firm in the one Spirit, striving together as one for the faith of the gospel without being frightened in any way by those who oppose you." (Philippians 1:27-28).

Holy Spirit, help us to live worthy of the Truth that is Jesus. Help us to be living testimonies of God's Love, His grace and mercy (Romans 12: 1-2).

- Father, help us to live for You, and let Your light shine through us (Matthew 5:16).
- Holy Spirit, help us to be bold, confident, and courageous to declare the goodness of the Lord and draw all men around us to God the Father.
- Holy Spirit, help us to be rooted in You, keep us united, to strengthen one another in the mission and purpose of establishing God's Kingdom here on earth.

"There are different kinds of gifts, but the same Spirit distributes them. There are different kinds of service, but the same Lord. There are different kinds of working, but in all of them and in everyone it is the same God at work." (1 Corinthians 12:4-6).

- Holy Spirit, thank You for the gifts You have bestowed on us, help us to steward them diligently and faithfully to the glory of God.
- Father, purge us of those things that bring discord, rivalry, self-promotion, and division, help us to lay personal agenda aside and focus on Your agenda, Your vision and Your purpose for the Church.

> "...Also, seek the peace and prosperity of the city to which I have carried you into exile. Pray to the LORD for it, because if it prospers, you too will prosper." (Jeremiah 29:7).

- Holy Spirit, activate us to be aligned to seek the prosperity of the Kingdom of God where we have been planted.
- Father, let Your Body be effective in delivering God's will, plan and purpose in the land You've established us in.
- Give us a Kingdom perspective of our communities, give us Your heart for the lives around us, reveal Kingdom strategies, responses, and solutions to the challenges in our communities.

Prayers for Spiritual Leaders: Protection, Wisdom, Grace

"Remember your leaders, who spoke the word of God to you." (Hebrews 13:7 NIV).

"Dear brothers and sisters, honour those who are your leaders in the Lord's work. They work hard among you and give you spiritual guidance. Show them great respect and wholehearted love because of their work. And live peacefully with each other." (1 Thessalonians 5:12 NIV).

Being a spiritual leader has been described as one of the toughest jobs on earth. It comes with great risks and challenges and is no doubt perhaps one of the most thankless jobs.

As children of God, we have a duty to care for our spiritual leaders and invest time praying scripture-based, faith-filled prayers for them. As the Body of Christ, their role is crucial to fulfilling God's plan and purpose, they are on the frontline of this mission, and we have a duty of care towards them. May God continue to keep us and bless us as we lovingly and dutifully pray for your spiritual leaders.

"But among you it will be different. Whoever wants to be a leader among you must be your servant." (Matthew 20:26 NLT).

- Jesus, I pray that You renew the strength of my spiritual leaders to serve You and the Church the way you do.
- Holy Spirit, help our church leaders to be rooted in You so much so that their lives stand out always – be their grace, strength, comfort and hope.

"Those who live in the shelter of the Most High will find rest in the shadow of the Almighty. This I declare about the Lord: He alone is my refuge, my place of safety; he is my God, and I trust him. For he will rescue you from every trap and protect you from deadly disease." (Psalm 91:1-2 NLT).

- Father, I pray that our spiritual leaders will abide in You and dwell in Your shelter.
- Father, grant our spiritual leaders rest. Refresh them, restore them, help them to live a life of trust and faith where they cast every burden on You and are not weighed down by the burdens of others.
- Father, lead our church leaders to a place of safety – spiritually, physically, financially, in their ministry and marriages. Protect their entire family from the snares and attacks of the enemy.
- Heavenly Father, protect our church leaders from the world. Help them to guard their hearts and minds from the corruption of this world so they may be filled with and can only pour out Your truth and love.

- Holy Spirit, keep our leaders under the shield of faith to protect them from the fiery darts of the enemy (Ephesians 6:16).

"...and do not give the devil a foothold." (Ephesians 4:26 NIV).

- Holy Spirit, help our spiritual leaders to walk in the light of God and to be covered all around.
- Holy Spirit, block every entry point through which the enemy may attack their lives, or gain entry into their lives.
- Father, shut down every demonic manipulation and corruption in the household and lives of our spiritual leaders.
- Have mercy and pour out Your grace and favour on our church leaders, purify and sanctify them so that Your power may flow through their lives.

"He allowed no one to oppress them; for their sake he rebuked kings: Do not touch my anointed ones; do my prophets no harm." (Psalm 105:14-15 NIV).

- Heavenly Father, deal with every attack against our spiritual leaders, rebuke every source of aggression, disruption, insecurity, and danger aimed at them. I declare their peace and safety in Jesus name.
- Give them the boldness to be Your voice, to fear and obey You.
- Help them to count the cost of serving You and to follow diligently and passionately.

"His master replied, Well done, good and faithful servant! You have been faithful with a few things; I will put you in charge of many things. Come and share your master's happiness!" (Matthew 25:21 NIV).

- Affirm them Lord; give them the assurances they

need to serve You. Lord, allow me to be a blessing to them in Jesus name.

• Provide for the vision you have birthed in their hearts, give them the heavenly and material resources needed to see it come to fruition in Jesus name.

• Holy Spirit, grant our spiritual leaders the grace, wisdom, knowledge and understanding to please the Lord at all times.

• Holy Spirit, grant our spiritual leaders the favour to multiply everything the Lord has placed in their hands – let them prosper in everything they do.

• Father, thank you for our spiritual leaders who have responded to Your call on their lives. Let them lack no good thing, let them live in comfort, peace and good health. Let their children and spouses excel and thrive in all things and dwell in the peace and safety of God. Thank You for their lives.

Section 7
Praise, Worship, Thanksgiving

"The Lord is my strength and my shield; in him my heart trusts, and I am helped; my heart exults, and with my song I give thanks to him." (Psalm 28:7).

- Lord, I declare that I will praise You, worship You and thank You even before I receive the breakthrough I'm hoping for.
- Thank You for the gift of faith and confidence of the things I hope for which are according to Your will. Thank You for the assurance of the things that I do not see (Hebrews 11:1 NIV).
- Lord, thank You because You will never leave me nor forsake me and I can put all my faith, hope and trust in You.
- Thank You because no matter how many promises You have made, they are 'Yes' in Christ. So Lord today I say thank You and Amen to everything You've spoken concerning me (2 Corinthians 1:20 NIV).

"Always be joyful. Never stop praying. Be thankful in all circumstances, for this is God's will for you who belong to Christ Jesus (1 Thessalonians 5:16-18 NIV).

- Thank You Father for being faithful and consistent. Holy Spirit, help my heart to be positioned in a place of gratitude and thanksgiving.
- Thank You Lord, that even in the midst of the storm,

you are there. You are the maker of the world and the universe, supreme ruler and authority, everything is in Your hands, I praise You because nothing is too big for You.
- I thank You, Lord, for my circumstances, I pray that every situation will glorify and please You.
- Thank You because I am Yours, adopted into Your family as Your child and I bear Your name – what an honour and privilege. Thank You, Jesus.

"Give thanks to the Lord, for he is good; his love endures forever." (1 Chronicles 16:34).
- Holy Spirit, open my eyes to see God in everything. Lord, I thank You because You really are good.
- Thank You Lord for Your enduring love. Help me Holy Spirit to experience God's love in full measure today. Let that experience empower and transform me.
- Thank You Lord because of the power of Your love for me, I receive it and embrace it.
- I'm grateful that Your love not only resides in me, it can flow through me; Holy Spirit, let me be a conduit through which this powerful love is expressed.

"For everything God created is good, and nothing is to be rejected if it is received with thanksgiving, because it is consecrated by the word of God and prayer." (1 Timothy 4:4-5).
- Thank You for Your provision, protection, favour and blessing.
- Thank You for everything you provide that I often take for granted... Lord, in this moment, I declare my gratitude for Your goodness and faithfulness.
- Lord, I receive everything You have prepared for me

with humility and thanksgiving; thank You because every day You make available everything that I need for a life of holiness and righteousness! Thank You, Lord (2 Peter 1:3).

"Do not be anxious about anything, but in every situation, by prayer and petition, with thanksgiving, present your requests to God. And the peace of God, which transcends all understanding, will guard your hearts and your minds in Christ Jesus." (Philippians 4:6-7).